Changing the Conversation: Volume II

21st Club presents a collection of insights for football club boardrooms

D1825302

"Intuitive, intelligent and insightful. Perfect reading for the modern game."
(Jeff Agoos, Senior VP, Major League Soccer)

"Always challenging established norms and pushing the boundaries."
(Daniel Geey, Partner, Sheridans Sports Group)

"A terrific read for those with an open mind! At Hibernian the conversation
has definitely changed!"
(George Craig, Head of Football Operations, Hibernian)

"Unless you are looking to think differently you will repeat the same
mistakes and create no competitive advantage. This book helped me
question things."
(Keith Wyness, CEO, Aston Villa)

"Data is too often used in the way in which a drunk uses lamp posts – for
support rather than illumination. 21st Club can be counted on to help make
what you're counting count."
(Ian Lynam, Founding Partner, Northridge Law LLP)

"Constantly, and wisely, challenging our assumptions about football."
(Matt Dickinson, Chief Sports Writer, The Times)

"Thought provoking reading, bringing fresh perspectives to solving
common football problems"
(Rebecca Caplehorn, Director of Football Operations, Tottenham Hotspur)

21st Club always inspire, challenge and provide a viewpoint different to
everyone else."
(Mike Rigg, Global Football Advisor, SRi)

"Fresh, analytical and thought-provoking."
(Dan Jones, Lead Partner, Deloitte Sports Business Group)

"Always encouraging insightful thought in bringing performance strategy to life."
(Steven Gunn, Director of Football Operations, Aberdeen)

"As always, an informative representation of facts challenging confirmation bias."
(Steve Curwood, CEO, Fleetwood Town)

"21st Club continually provide new ways of thinking about football's oldest problems."
(Sean Ingle, Senior Sports Writer, The Guardian)

"Incredible data and insight. A must-have to understand modern football."
(Murad Ahmed, Leisure Correspondent, Financial Times)

"Ideas that show us that other football is possible."
(Alex Aranzabal, Former President, S.D. Eibar)

"Once again a real thought-provoking read that makes you assess and challenge all your thinking."
(Paul Mitchell, Head of Recruitment, RB Leipzig)

"The innovators bringing smartness to football."
(Simon Mesfin, Sports Director, Lillestrøm Sportsklubb)

"A cross from a completely different angle."
(Ivan Kepčija, Technical Director, Legia Warszawa SA)

"Useful insights to enhance decision making off the pitch."
(Emilio Gutierez, Director, Girona FC)

"Critical perspectives for the executives of modern day football."
(Kaan Öz, Board Member, Göztepe S.K.)

"Valuable and thought-provoking insight. Helps you see the game from a different perspective."
(David Court, Talent ID & Development Education Lead, The FA)

"The insight is extremely relevant and the slightly different perspective is refreshing."
(Mal Brannigan, CEO, Dundalk FC)

Contents

Acknowledgements

The creation of this book has been a collaborative project between the 21st Club team and our network of colleagues and contributors.

21st Club's Omar Chaudhuri, Ben Marlow and Blake Wooster have produced the majority of insights featured in this book. However, we would like to extend our thanks for the valuable contributions from Liam Grant, Chris Mann and Luis Usier, all of whom have written with great enthusiasm and wisdom on their chosen subjects.

Thanks also to Chris Mann for managing the editorial process, Elizabeth Marlow for her work on the cover design, and to Opta Sports for supplying performance data.

Introduction

21st Club stands for the spirit of winning by thinking differently. **Not only is it more fun to out-think rather than out-spend the competition, it also makes more sense.** Achieving success in this way means a more attractive, profitable and sustainable football club.

Five years ago we started to serve those like-minded souls in the game with smart tools and fresh concepts to challenge the received wisdoms that can hinder progress. A movement was started that became a catalyst for a new way of thinking in football. The conversation *is* changing, and we are proud to be a part of the more ambitious and strategic boardroom culture that is taking hold.

We feel privileged to be in position where we are inside the game, yet also able to observe it by offering an 'outside view'. As such, we're able to take a unique perspective that recognises the inefficiencies in football while understanding the inherent forces that drive them.

The first volume of *Changing the Conversation* was published after reaching a milestone of 100 posts on our weekly blog – a series of articles that were designed to help our audience see problems from a different perspective and find a better way. The feedback showed us there was a critical mass curious and hungry for fresh perspective. That call to action has prompted us to release a follow-up in celebration of another 21st Club landmark, our five-year anniversary.

This latest edition follows the same structure as its predecessor, bringing together a selection of our most popular articles and grouping them into four main chapters:

1. Strategy
2. Talent
3. Performance, and
4. Planning

Presenting some of the stories, case studies and statistical models that we've created and discovered along the way, this paperback is perfect as a coffee table addition or pocket-size travel companion. We hope you enjoy the read and that our work gives you the confidence and courage to see your everyday challenges in a new light as you shape the future of your organisations.

As we embark on the next phase of our own business, we continue to seek out collaborations with clubs, leagues, federations and investors who share our curiosity for finding the next competitive edge and have the bravery to execute before their rivals.

If that sounds like you, then we'd love to hear from you.

I: STRATEGY

Help Me, Help You

Rod Tidwell stands naked, his inquisitive look the reaction to the imploring face of his agent, Jerry Maguire. "Help me, help you," Maguire repeats, over and over, his red face framing the exasperation in his eyes. Help me, help you.

This is the seminal moment in the film, Jerry Maguire. The moment where Tidwell, played by an inspired Cuba Gooding Jr., finally listens to the man who has staked everything on his career. This is Maguire's last roll of the dice – his final, desperate attempt to free Tidwell from the distraction of his next contract to enable him to focus on his next performance, his next game, his next opportunity to showcase his ability to the world. For failure to perform on the pitch would render any contract aspirations redundant.

Such is the challenge of professional sport. With the world watching at the weekend, each performance is critical to validating your work. Judgement is swift and opinions can change in the time it takes for a ball to cross the goal line. With such pressure, the next match is not a distraction but the focal point.

Herein lies the challenge. In football, we need to be constantly re-laying the foundations for the future while also doing everything that we can to win the next game. Yet it is almost impossible for club boardrooms to scan the horizon effectively while also watching their step.

Such is the value of an outside view. Seeking help from outside of the club can provide much-needed bandwidth while also ensuring that the prevailing thinking within the club is constructively challenged to deliver the best possible outcome in the long run.

Unencumbered by social proofing, a designated 'Red Team' that helps to look after the future of your club will not help you win this weekend (that's your job), but it will help you win in the future. Knowing that will make achievements in the short term all the sweeter.

Punching Above Your Weight

During the past few years, the likes of Uber and Lyft have roared into town to challenge the traditional taxicab industry, Spotify have done to iTunes what iTunes did to CDs, while Slack is busy revolutionising the way that organisations communicate. With relatively fewer resources at their inception, these companies have been able to outthink and outmaneuver their more established rivals in a short space of time.

We see similar disruption in football, where certain clubs have recently demonstrated that money isn't the only differentiator. Leicester City shocked the world in 2015/16 by executing a playing style that rivals found hard to stifle. Clubs like Dinamo Zagreb continue to demonstrate their ability to balance youth development with repeated Champions League qualification. In Spain, Atlético Madrid's succession planning process has enabled them to replace Fernando Torres, with Sergio Agüero, with Radamel Falcao, with Diego Costa, and now Antoine Griezemann, while remaining fiercely competitive in an unbalanced league. In Italy, Atalanta accumulated more than €30m of income from player trading between 2011/12 and 2014/15, yet still significantly outperform many wealthier Serie A rivals.

Paradoxically, having tasted success, these market-leading companies and clubs are now relatively cash rich and so face a whole new challenge: how to avoid complacency and maintain success.

So, if access to resources are not the only differentiator, then suddenly the challenge becomes less about the resources that constrain us and more about the thinking that can propel us.

And then the conversation changes again: what are we willing to do differently in order to get an edge on our rivals?

Dare to Be Different

"BOWLED! Stephen Harmison with a slower ball, one of the great balls! Given the moment, given the batsman, and given the match that is a staggering gamble that has paid off for Harmison."

There is palpable excitement in cricket commentator Mark Nicholas' voice as England bowler Stephen Harmison's unusual delivery cannons into the batsman's stumps during the second match of the 2005 Ashes series. It was a must-win match, with England trailing by one in the series, but the truth is that Harmison wasn't taking a 'staggering gamble' at all. Regardless of the outcome of that ball, England would still have been firm favourites to win.

The fact that it was both different and the stakes were high meant that the perception of the risk outweighed the reality. It was seen as risky simply because it was different.

In football, we see this all the time. With relegation prevalent, the stakes are too high to risk making a mistake. Going down can sometimes have lasting, existential consequences, the fear of which can stifle our willingness to leave the herd, innovation only coming when financial pressure or other limitations force our hand. We therefore stick to what we know.

Interestingly, MLS and other closed leagues offer an environment shorn of this fear, creating an ideal testbed for experimentation where one poor season is the worst that can happen. City Football Group's ownership of New York City is interesting in this respect, as it provides a safe environment to try things – Patrick Vieira's apprenticeship being a good example. Owners may wish to consider multiple-club ownership to take advantage of this when devising strategies for the future.

Not everyone has this luxury, however, meaning that to do something different in more traditional leagues requires a certain type of bravery. Bravery to ignore potential ridicule. Bravery to accept that the reaction to any failure is likely to be exacerbated. But the rewards are there for those who try.

In truth, Harmison was not taking a 'staggering gamble' but a calculated risk. Knowing what we stand to gain as well as what we may lose can help us to do the same and in mustering the bravery to execute, we may have a chance of achieving beyond our own expectations.

The Profit-Utility Trade-Off

As a sports owner or director of a team it is crucial to know the purpose of our organisation. Are we there to make a profit, or are we there to win trophies? The ideal answer would of course be both, but whilst everyone could be profitable, not everyone can be a winner.

The theory behind how these two forces interact in sport has long been established. Academic research reflecting on the nature of North American and European sport – and our own experience with clubs – has outlined the competing camps of profit-maximisation versus utility-maximisation (i.e. winning trophies). In a nutshell, the theory tells us that pursuing profit in a utility environment means you get left behind; pursuing utility will ultimately be unsustainable for most people.

Clearly the question is: how can this theory help us in practice?

The sporting world, especially in Europe, is moving toward a more nuanced environment where the interaction between profit and utility is ever more complex. To be able to plan and thrive in this dynamic world the starting point is a clear definition of your goals.

A rounded understanding of the fundamentals of theory can help develop a sense of what might be realistic to aim for and what the eventual consequences may be. Is it acceptable to our organisation that protecting the balance sheet may come at a cost to the trophy cabinet? Is the attempt at increasing your chances of success worth the risk to the long-term health of the organisation? A good recent example of this is FC Porto. A bold rebuilding plan in the pursuit of trophies dramatically increased their losses and has endangered their ability to compete in future seasons.

We have already seen this issue recognised by UEFA with the introduction of Financial Fair Play regulations. However, ultimate responsibility lies with individual organisations. If we can form and answer the types of questions above, we can better understand what our purpose really is and position ourselves to succeed within this frame.

The Cost of a Contract

In December 2016, investigations by The Sunday Times revealed some of the finer details of bonuses within players' contracts. While perhaps not a surprise to those working inside the game, the revelations provoked much discussion about their influence on player behaviour.

The truth is that these clauses are the final details in the lengthy and often costly process of recruiting a player. We expend a great deal of energy trying to acquire talent, and it is difficult to ignore this significant sunk cost during the latter stages of negotiations.

There are ways, however, to avoid sunk-cost bias in contract negotiations. The first is to ensure the club has clear principles around its fixed and variable cost structures, for example those set out by Ferran Soriano during his time at Barcelona. Of course this is easier when running a club that has limited competition in talent acquisition, but nevertheless having structures that are clearly articulated to the market can help eliminate potential signings earlier in the process.

The second is to keep options open and never be fooled into thinking that any one player is the 'perfect' option. We know that as many of half of new signings will not even become 'core' first team players; there are many unknowns in recruitment.

In football, these are the two biggest forces that can increase buyer power in contract negotiations. Getting these processes working can produce more, comparable options for the same cost, or reduce the total cost of signing players altogether.

The Joy of Misplaced Optimism

It never ceases to amaze us as to why footballers choose to shoot so regularly from outside the penalty area, when less than 4 in 100 of these attempts are scored.

Or why top-division clubs continue to use a substantial amount of scarce resource into scouting lower and weaker leagues for peak-age players, when the relative meritocracy of football means that the possibility of finding a 'diamond in the rough' is becoming diminishingly small.

Or, outside of football, why millions of people play the lottery or gamble, even though the losses each year can be hugely material.

Traditional economic theory would have this behaviour as irrational, or at the very least sub-optimal. However, the advances made by Daniel Kahneman and Amos Tversky mean we now understand why people pursue low probability outcomes.

Part of the reason is that there is a different type of joy from low-probability successes. A 30-yard screamer just feels better to the scorer than a clumsy tap-in, even though the outcome is the same. A club wins more plaudits for signing a player no one else appeared to identify, compared to a club that took wisdom from the crowd and secured a more sought-after, but equally productive player.

We also tend to overestimate the probability of success from these events, for the very reason that they are memorable. Highlights programmes show just a tiny fraction of the 3,000+ long-range attempts that fly wide, are blocked or saved in any given season, but the ones that do go in stick in the mind. In recruitment, Jamie Vardy's success disguises the fact that most peak-age signings who step up even one division, let alone two or three, struggle to excel, and at a cost that can easily sum up to that of signings from major leagues.

But football needn't be a series of long shots. There is data and research that can enable us to identify strategies that bring both more success and less variance.

Why try to beat the odds when you can move them in your favour?

Talking The Talk

The football industry is going through a period of change in which establishing joined-up football services off the pitch is a key strategic goal and often a major logistical challenge.

To be able to succeed in this respect and introduce the new ideas that are central to its advancement requires a certain bravery on the part of those guiding the project. Without this courage there will inevitably be difficulties when old ideas are brought into direct conflict with the new. At best this situation leads to a simple and temporary misunderstanding; at worst it invokes open hostility and the rejection of potentially important work.

It is hardly novel to say that communication is key to processes such as these, and yet the tools that enable an exchange of ideas in an accurate and succinct manner are often underdeveloped. We are not talking about a stubborn reliance on outdated technology, but something more fundamental — the basic concepts and language we use when talking about our aims.

A potential approach is to develop an internal vernacular around certain topics (or at least foster the conditions for this to occur). Establishing a simple set of words or phrases that describe the most common issues or those that are most fundamental to a task can provide the broad references needed to help bridge the gap between old and new. For example, when attempting to discuss a broad concept like the creativity of a player, having a way to explicitly describe the various aspects that avoids jargon can help everyone frame what is being discussed. Bracketing the type of play that involves receiving the ball high up the pitch and playing a forward pass as Type X play, rather than defining it by the various metrics that might have been used to measure it, helps quickly convey a specific context. With that established, we can then focus on the finer details of the discussion.

Clearly this is not a quick and easy solution and would require a committed uptake. However, such an approach need not be a complete reinvention of language; many of us already use this idea casually. If a more formal focus is first given to establishing this common language it can also help set the culture of organisations. The approach is flexible and will by definition be suited to the specific demands of our task. Crucially, if successful it can also shift attention to broader strategic goals rather than short-term problem solving.

The Distant GM

The ability to remain objective and view information dispassionately is central to any robust decision-making process. At 21st Club we frequently expound the benefits of getting an 'outside view' when setting strategic objectives or making other major decisions. But what if clubs went further and more fully incorporated the role of 'the outsider' into their organisational culture?

During an appearance on The Bill Simmons Podcast in March 2017, the author Malcolm Gladwell proposed the idea of the 'Distant GM'. Gladwell's suggestion was that sports teams would be able to make better decisions if one or more key executives were intentionally removed from the day-to-day running of the organisation. Rather than being involved in the routine management of the club, these individuals would be geographically separated from the team and only be called upon when required to support key strategic decisions. The objectivity afforded them by their distance would be their greatest asset.

The reasoning behind Gladwell's theory is that 'distant' executives would be shielded from the hundreds of unconscious biases that we accumulate when we work inside an organisation. These biases, be they system justification or emotional relationships, can significantly impair judgement and prevent clubs from making the most effective decisions. For example, a distant GM would be able to negotiate player contracts without having formed subjective judgements of individuals, or restructure departments without loyalty to processes implemented by others within the club.

The appointment of a distant GM might seem like a radical and unprecedented step, but the objectivity offered by such a position has the potential to bring far greater levels of impartiality to the boardroom. As clubs constantly strive to become more efficient and equitable in their business operations, such a role could become commonplace within – or rather without – organisations in the years to come.

The Breadth-Depth Compromise

In an ideal world we would scout every footballer on the planet and have full knowledge of each player's suitability for our club. However, limited resources mean we have to strike a compromise between the breadth and depth of our search:

1. Prioritise breadth: by scouting many players, we reduce the risk of missing out on talent, but this might mean we make poor decisions based on limited information.

2. Prioritise depth: by being more selective about the players, teams and leagues we scout we gain a deep understanding of the suitability of these players, but risk missing out on some talent.

This problem is illustrated below, with Club A striking a balance between the two.

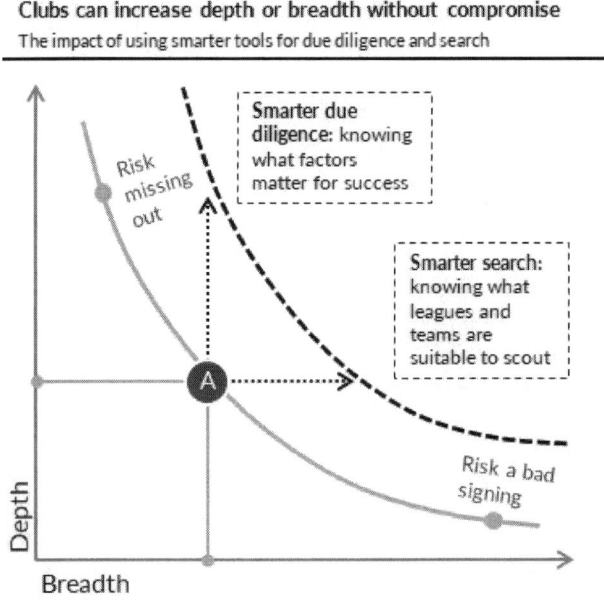

Smarter tools can – for any given breadth of search – increase the depth with which you can assess potential signings. This might include having a better understanding of what is important for success in their league, meaning that due diligence can focus on clear, specific factors around the player.

Club A can also reduce the chances of missing out on a player. Say they only have the resources to watch 300 players to a certain level of detail in any given season. Smarter information around search – such as knowing which teams or competitions produce suitable players for their league – means they can increase their effective breadth of search as they have fewer unsuitable players on their radar.

Both the thought of a bad signing and of missing out on a player are powerful forces when we make decisions around the allocation of resources in player recruitment. While the risk of both will never be fully eliminated, smarter tools can make us more efficient in both the search and due diligence process.

Because Thinking Is Hard

In football there are cognitive biases that can hinder our better judgement when recruiting new players. For example, we might overvalue experience – because know-how feels safe and so we assume it's important – or be overly optimistic about a new player because we desperately want the signing to work out.

Recently, we came across this handy cognitive bias cheat sheet courtesy of Buster Benson, Platform Product Lead at Slack, who's set to write a book around these topics.

COGNITIVE BIAS CHEAT SHEET
BECAUSE THINKING IS HARD

1 TOO MUCH INFO
SO ONLY NOTICE...
- CHANGES
- BIZARRENESS
- REPETITION
- CONFIRMATION

2 NOT ENOUGH MEANING
SO FILL IN GAPS WITH...
- PATTERNS
- GENERALITIES
- BENEFIT OF DOUBT
- EASIER PROBLEMS
- OUR CURRENT MINDSET

3 NOT ENOUGH TIME
SO ASSUME...
- WE'RE RIGHT
- WE CAN DO THIS
- NEAREST THING IS BEST
- FINISH WHAT'S STARTED
- KEEP OPTIONS OPEN
- EASIER IS BETTER

4 NOT ENOUGH MEMORY
SO SAVE SPACE BY...
- EDITING MEMORIES DOWN
- GENERALIZING
- KEEPING AN EXAMPLE
- USING EXTERNAL MEMORY

BY BENSON.
HTTP://BIT.LY/THINKING-IS-HARD

Benson's cheat sheet points to four common scenarios that lead to biased thinking. Consider them in a player trading context: sometimes we have too much information to process, so we many only end up noticing a player's memorable but unrepresentative moments, like tournament performance or goals scored against our club. Conversely, when there's not enough meaning in the information we tend to fill the gaps with assumptions based on our current mindset, like our own perceptions of value in experience.

When there's not enough memory we tend to save space by generalising or remembering the outliers (the exception to success, rather than the norm). When there's not enough time – perhaps the most applicable scenario in a football context – we're more likely to assume that we're right about a player and so execute the transaction without proper due diligence.

Objective thinking is hard and so – to protect against cognitive biases in player trading – we developed our Acquisition tool. By enabling quick yet comprehensive player due diligence, Acquisition helps clubs mitigate risk and maximise success in the transfer market.

Chart: https://medium.com/@buster

The Importance of Self-Awareness

In a May 2017 article for The Guardian, Oliver Burkeman reported on some of the work being done by Tasha Eurich, an organisational psychologist, author and expert on the subject of self-awareness.

According to Eurich, 95% of people *think* they're self-aware but only 10-15% of us really *are*. If we're not self-aware then we only have a limited understanding our own motivations and the ways in which we are perceived by others.

In order to better understand ourselves, Eurich recommends asking *'what'* questions rather than simply wondering *'why'* things happen to us. Asking *'why'* questions (e.g. "Why did I fail my exam?") tends to lead us to speculate and construct false narratives around our experiences, while asking 'what' (e.g. "What was it about my preparation that caused me to fail the exam?") can help us to identify patterns of behaviour that can be analysed and changed.

In a football context, we can apply similar lines of thinking to strategic decision-making within our club. Wrapped up in the everyday business of running an organisation, it is possible become short-sighted and lose objectivity regarding our own processes. By falling into comfortable habits or having misplaced confidence in the power of our intuition, we can make ourselves blind to reality and take poor decisions as a result.

This myopia can manifest itself in a number of ways. If we're over-reliant on our instincts, then we might be too quick to approve or discard a potential signing without getting a more objective view of their true performance level. If we're short on time, then we might settle for a deal without completing the appropriate level of due diligence. Being blind to our own limitations in this way only serves to perpetuate a cycle of poor decision-making.

In player recruitment, rather than starting with "Why did that player not succeed at our club?" and proceeding to build false narratives around events, we should instead ask "What was it about the player's performance that wasn't considered good enough for our club?"

Lessons from The NBA

The recently completed 2016/17 NBA season was the first to pass without a single head coach being fired since 1970/71. Given that the league saw 18 in-season sackings between 2012 and 2016, the current stability of NBA coaching jobs is unprecedented in the modern era. It remains to be seen whether 2016/17 will stand as an outlier, but the recent stalling of the NBA's coaching carousel is an interesting phenomenon.

As of the end of the 2016/17 season, the median NBA coach had been in his job for 2.1 years, compared to just 11 months in England, Germany and Spain's top football divisions. While the European leagues have the added threat of relegation, the longevity of many NBA coaches in similarly pressurised environments could be interpreted as a sign that franchises have improved processes regarding the recruitment and performance measurement of coaches.

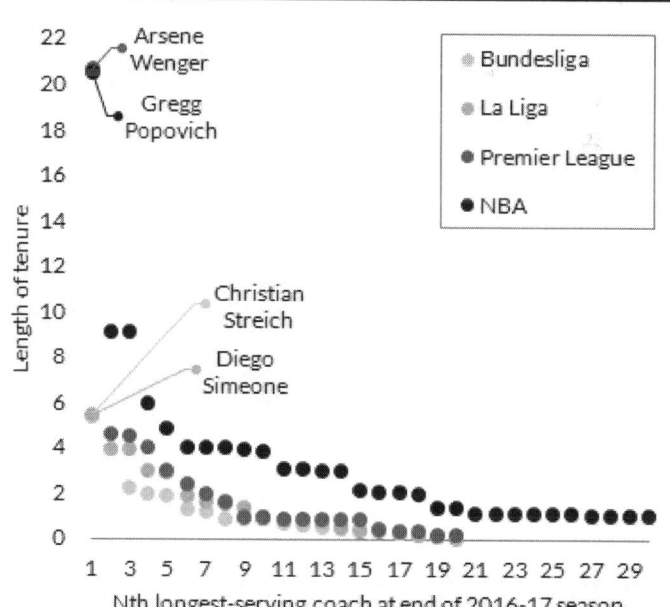

NBA coaching tenures are far longer than those in football
Head coach time in job at end of 2016-17 season, longest tenures highlighted

In football it can be easy to fall into the trap of expending a huge amount of effort ensuring that we get our player transfers right, only to fall short of the same standards when it comes to managerial appointments. Often we see clubs assemble expensive playing squads only to hire a manager who is a poor fit from a technical and philosophical perspective. If we don't conduct the appropriate levels of due diligence when hiring a manager, then we are setting ourselves up for failure and a cycle of instability.

Over the last few years, Southampton have generally been a good example of a football club that uses extensive due diligence to ensure continuity in its managerial appointments. Despite having managers poached by other clubs, Southampton have maintained a clear idea of the type of manager that fits their overall strategy and have generally been able to identify suitable candidates in advance by measuring their performance against relevant KPIs.

Asking even the simplest of questions can give us a better chance of finding the right candidates and avoiding purely reactive appointments. If we want to promote players from our academy, then we need to assess a coach's track record in developing young talent. If we are committed to a particular type of football, then we need a manager who has had success with a similar style. Every piece of information we can gather, no matter how big or small, serves to validate our decisions and improve our chances of sustainable success.

Coaching stability such as that currently being enjoyed in the NBA is extremely rare, but we don't necessarily have to keep the same manager in place to retain a level continuity. Sometimes poor results or the elective departure of a coach obligate change, but that shouldn't stop us from sticking to our principles and using a comprehensive due diligence process to identify the managers most likely to deliver on our core objectives.

Definitely Probably

In 1964, the CIA's Sherman Kent tried to bridge the gap between 'poets' and 'mathematicians' when discussing the likelihood of certain events. He proposed that a phrase like 'probable' should represent an event with a 75% chance of taking place, while a phrase like 'we doubt' should be around a 30% chance.

His study inspired a number of polls, including the one below, about the probability people assign to certain phrases. For example, a typical person assigns a value of 90% to the term 'highly likely', though answers might range from 70% to 98%.

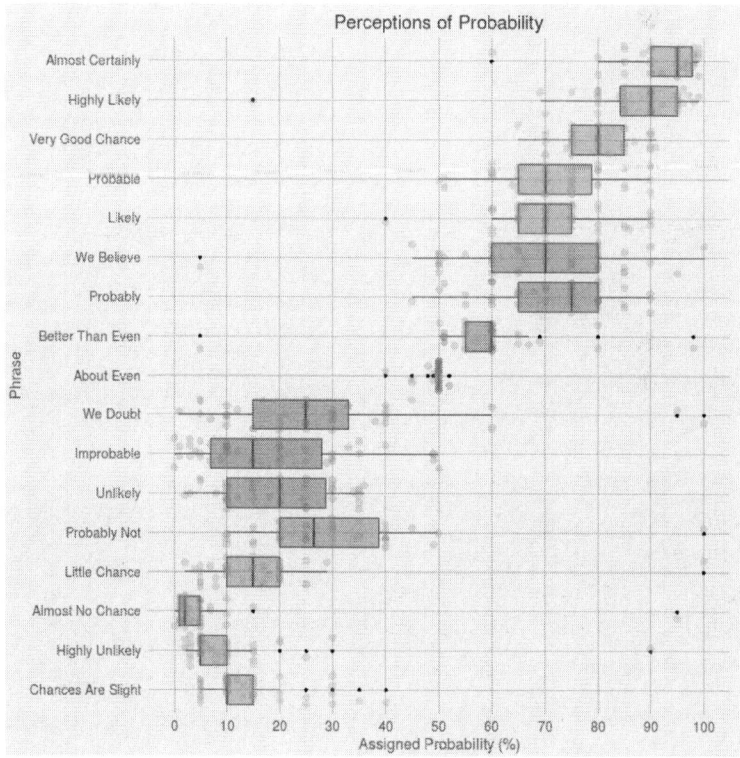

This is interesting in football because we deal with a number of uncertain outcomes. If, for example, we suggest an academy player would 'probably not' become a first team player at our club, it is important to bear in mind that the audience (his parents, the academy manager, the first team coach) could understand this as representing anything from a 1-in-5 chance to a 2-in-5 chance. Or if 'we believe' a potential new signing will hit certain objective benchmarks, the perception could range from 60% to 80%.

This might feel like splitting hairs, but it's important to establish a common language when discussing uncertainties. Indeed, failure to do so could lead to misunderstandings of expectations and costly mistakes – like overpaying on a new signing because of a misalignment on what a 'very good chance' of success actually meant.

There is of course no time more uncertain than the summer months, so having joined-up thinking on what's probable, possible, and unlikely, can ensure any recruitment decisions are made with clarity of thought.

Chart: https://www.reddit.com/user/zonination

Bean Bags and Sleeping Pods

The ultimate goal for any company – in or outside of football – is to achieve the highest possible returns for the lowest possible cost. A key factor in delivering this has been the ability to attract and retain better talent than your competitors. This is perhaps more true of sport than any other industry given the visibility of results.

Historically, this has involved simply paying more than anyone else. Today, however, companies are increasingly turning to culture to attract the top people. Google are perhaps the standard-bearer for 'cultural differentiation' with their campus-based offices, in-house chefs, bean bags and sleeping pods proving an effective means to keep their staff engaged.

But in football we are still generally trying to differentiate ourselves by the depth of our pockets, assuming players are only interested in what they can earn.

For the top teams, we predict that simply paying more will become increasingly ineffective at attracting talent. We already hear of players being prepared to take a cut in wages in return for more playing time, or for Champions League football (Alex Oxlade-Chamberlain being relatively a recent example). This presents an opportunity for smart clubs to differentiate themselves by cultivating a sense of achievement and belonging that numbers alone cannot afford.

This may go some way to explaining Tottenham Hotspur's current ability to punch above their financial weight.

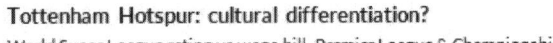

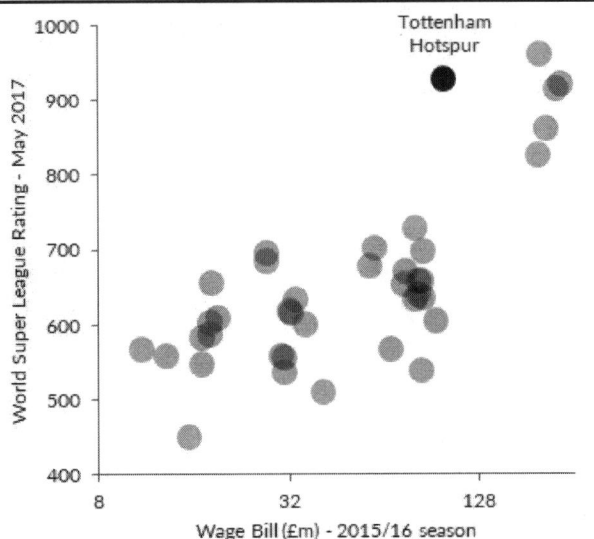

Tottenham Hotspur: cultural differentiation?
World Super League rating vs wage bill, Premier League & Championship

In our analysis of team strength relative to wages as calculated by 21st Club's World Super League, Tottenham are the clear outlier – achieving performances that are broadly in line with the other top six teams but at a much lower cost.

The club are clearly on a journey – they have lofty aspirations, an exciting new stadium in development, a young, high-quality squad and a dynamic coach. That the club have retained players capable of this level of performance suggests that they are bought into the vision and are there for more than just money. They want to see where the journey ends.

There are obviously challenges with this, and Kyle Walker's move to a direct rival was a stark reminder that money still talks. But through their culture, Tottenham are perhaps proving that return doesn't have to be solely financial.

The Motivated Player

Arjen Robben retired from international football back in October 2017. With the Netherlands having failed to qualify for the 2018 World Cup, Robben finished on 96 caps and therefore did not become the ninth Dutchman to reach a century of national appearances.

History tells us that this is unusual: of 52 now-retired players to have reached 90 caps for leading European countries, just 13 have not reached 100, with more finishing just above the milestone than just below. Logic, and the trend of players below, dictates that the inverse should be true, but clearly most players would rather not end their career just short of this nice, round number.

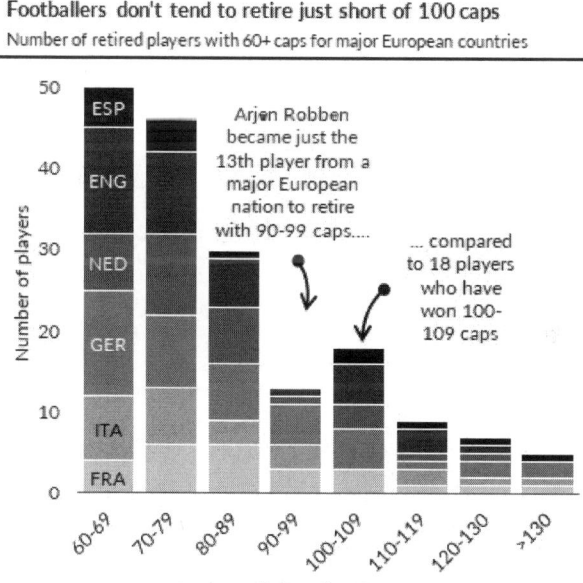

Footballers don't tend to retire just short of 100 caps
Number of retired players with 60+ caps for major European countries

Arjen Robben became just the 13th player from a major European nation to retire with 90-99 caps....

... compared to 18 players who have won 100-109 caps

Number of players

ESP ENG NED GER ITA FRA

60-69 70-79 80-89 90-99 100-109 110-119 120-130 >130

Number of international caps won

This suggests that footballers – like the rest of us – are clearly motivated by personal achievement, even when no financial reward is directly at stake. In some cases, this might even come at the detriment of the team (there is evidence of this in cricket, for example), but smart clubs can exploit this behaviour to their advantage.

Do we know, for example, what personal motivations our players have? Perhaps a player wants to become the team's regular free kick taker. Maybe he wants to grow his personal brand, or he wants to develop his own way of thinking about the game so that he can debate with and challenge his coaches.

There is no need to provide financial incentives around these achievements – the players have the innate motivation to pursue them. Instead, we can try to understand how we can help them achieve their goals, thereby creating motivated players who enjoy what they are doing and want to play for our club.

A Zero-Sum Game

There is an old (and frankly pretty weak) joke about two campers who are confronted by a bear. On assessing their predicament, one of the campers quietly starts to put on his trainers, removing his heavy walking boots in the process. The other asks, with incredulity, "Surely you don't think you can outrun that bear?"

"I don't have to," comes the response. "I only have to outrun you".

In football, we are constantly striving for that silver bullet that will propel us up the league table. As a result, we strive for perfection, and if we can't achieve it we have a tendency to stick with what we have.

But football is a zero-sum game. For us to win a greater number of games, other teams have to lose. Perfection shouldn't be the target. We should simply aim to be better than those against whom we compete. This is what will give us an edge.

Generally, those who achieve an edge on the pitch are those who are prepared to do something different off it. For example, this could be through taking a different approach to recruitment, hiring a head coach, remunerating our players or allocating our scouts.

Often, an edge can even come from simply adopting new approaches slightly faster than the rest.

Either way, doing something different might give us with trainers while the rest labour in walking boots.

Kasparov's Law

In 1997, IBM's chess-playing computer, Deep Blue, became the first machine to beat a world champion, in Garry Kasparov. Since then, computers have become part of the fabric of the game, competing in tournaments as well as providing training assistance for players.

'Freestyle' tournaments have also grown in popularity, where humans compete both with and against computers. The results of these tournaments have been a little surprising; while a combination of a human consulting a computer for help generally beat a computer playing solo, a chess grandmaster with a weak process for using their computer generally lost to an amateur player with a strong process for using their computer. This slightly counter-intuitive conclusion has been dubbed Kasparov's Law.

The parallels with football are clear. Take the recruitment of players or managers:

Kasparov's law can be applied to football from chess

Chess	Football
A computer playing alone generally loses to...	A statistical model that chooses which players to buy would generally do worse than...
... a chess grandmaster using a computer, but with a poor process. Who generally loses to...	... a highly knowledgeable team that uses data, but poorly. Who generally do worse than...
... a weaker human player using a computer, but with a strong process	... a moderately knowledgeable team with a strong process for using data

While football is nowhere near as precise as chess, intelligent analysis of data reveals consistent themes for success – whether in recruitment, game strategy, succession planning, and so on. This is no different to a chess computer suggesting moves that improve the chances of success.

The key, however, is to get this process right. Knowing how to use the data in a smart way can triumph over both superior knowledge and the most advanced statistical models. Rather than using data to confirm our own biases, it is best used to both guide and challenge our decision-making.

Unlike chess, football's own version of Kasparov's Law won't be played out in matches and tournaments – it'll be for smart boardrooms to exploit as competitive edge.

That Winning Feeling

There's the story of a football club that wanted to learn more about their supporters' matchday experience. After each game, they asked a selection of match-going fans what they thought of the atmosphere during the game, the view from their seat, their ease of buying food and drink, and so on. They asked the fans to score each area out of ten.

The club also asked their supporters how they would rate their journey to the match – was it easy to get to and into the stadium? Across all matches this question produced an average response of 6.3 out of 10; neither good nor bad. After defeats, however, the average rating was 4.8, and after wins an impressive 7.2. Fans' memories of their journey to the stadium were – seemingly irrationally – coloured by their experience of the match itself.

It's feasible that angry fans after defeats consciously scored every area lowly in order to vent their frustration at the club. Nevertheless, there are parallels with how we react to victories and defeats within our own roles. For example, we often get excited about a new signing, but then six months later find a reason ('didn't settle in', 'didn't suit our style of play') to explain why it didn't work out.

These reasons may be true, but they are mostly empty statements unless; a) they can be anticipated before events unfold, and b) actioned upon. In other words, we need to be making predictions and tracking whether they come true.

In the case of a new signing – who we know probably has close to a 50% chance of success – we should identify the areas that could go wrong, make a note, and see what we can do about them. Misremembering the past might be fine for matchday fans, but for football clubs it can mean a lack of planning for major decisions.

The Squad Behind the Squad

In January, our focus is often on investing in players who can help us win in the short-term. However, it is investment in non-playing staff that ultimately creates the processes and culture that drive sustainable success.

Investing in non-playing staff is rarely straightforward. Firstly, there's the pressure to win the next game – and that's mostly down to the players we've bought or developed. Secondly, talent in non-playing staff is less observable than talent in playing staff, so it can be hard to hire the right people.

What is apparent though is that leagues – and by extension clubs – who invest more in non-playing staff also tend to have more young players, who generally cost less (below).

The Netherlands – and to a lesser extent Scandinavian countries are good examples of this. The clubs in these leagues could choose to tilt their wage bill towards their playing squad, taking from their non-playing budget to afford the salaries that peak-age players demand. Instead – and unlike clubs in Turkey, Russia or Greece – they keep their squads young and relative investment in non-playing staff high.

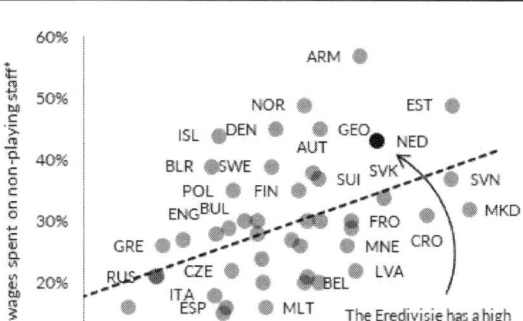

Having a young squad frees up cash for non-playing staff
% of wages on non-playing staff vs % of players who are under 23, Europe

The Eredivisie has a high % of wages spent on non-playing staff than- possibly helped by it's high % of under-23 players

% of playing time by U23s, 2017-18

*Source: UEFA Benchmarking Report

The benefits to this approach are clear. Not only are clubs creating value by developing young players, they are also investing in people that can protect the long-term future of the club. What's more, the return on investment from an extra member of non-playing staff can sometimes exceed that of an extra member of the playing squad, particularly when we consider the limited amount of minutes some individuals play.

Of course, on-field circumstances vary, meaning some clubs need to increase spending on their playing squad for certain periods of time. After all, there's no use having the world's best backroom team if you have the world's worst playing eleven! However, some clubs are spending over 40% of their wage budget on non-playing staff, and this seems to go hand-in-hand with a more sustainable approach to squad management.

The Right Science

There is a lot that we can learn from seeing how the same challenges are faced and resolved in different contexts. We often look to other industries to identify whether there are any approaches that may be applied to football.

An asset management company when hiring a fund manager, for example, will seek out a combination of both objective and subjective information to help them make the best decision possible. Subjective information is sought through references and rigorous interviews (art), while objective performance measures are available through assessing a candidate's past performance from the funds they have managed (science). This provides a full spectrum of information on which to make a decision, resulting in a better chance of success.

In football, we have been adopting a similar art/science approach to recruitment. We recognise the value in traditional methods of assessing talent through the experienced and often expert judgement of scouts, but we are also aware of objective information that can be used to further enhance the quality of our decisions.

The appetite is already there to enhance our processes with a little science, but the challenge is in establishing what 'a little science' actually means. Sometimes, the temptation is to throw as many statistics as possible into the mix, but this can actually create more confusion than clarity. Other times it can be to completely ignore it in favour of more familiar turf, with some clubs incorrectly believing that it is either/or.

The key is to identify the right science by establishing which information is most correlated with success. This may often result in eschewing more 'cutting edge' metrics in favour of simple, yet critical criteria. Things like team strength, playing time and age, for example, remain the biggest indicators of success when recruiting players according to the data, and clubs whose recruitment is driven by these factors, among others, are likely to outperform those whose aren't.

We are continually evolving our approach to recruitment. Supplementing the art with the right science can help make it a positive evolution for all.

II: TALENT

What Could Possibly Go Wrong?

The hiring of a new manager or head coach always brings renewed hope and expectation. There's talk of 'fresh ideas' and a 'clean slate', and most teams enjoy a rebound in results from the previous regime (even if this is mostly regression to the mean).

However, we know that in major European leagues, 8 out of 10 managers do not reach their two-year anniversary. Along the line – and usually sooner rather than later – we know that it will probably go wrong. This shouldn't be a surprise to us, so there's no excuse not to be prepared.

So what can clubs do to anticipate and preempt potential managerial issues?

1. Track performance. In 2014 we highlighted how Newcastle's slump in results was in spite of good performances, and that they were unlikely to remain 19th in the league (see the first volume of *Changing the Conversation*). They duly went unbeaten for the next six games with the same manager.

2. Keep clear lines of communication. Articulating clear targets for the incumbent manager – whether around results, youth opportunities or recruitment – ensures that any review process can be performed objectively.

3. Search more efficiently. Identify managers whose style, substance and resourcefulness would be an ideal fit should the worst happen.

4. Crystalise the club's philosophy. Doing this enables clubs to determine exactly what they want from their next manager or head coach.

Whether the season is yet to begin or well underway, there's never a bad time to start preparing for what could possibly go wrong.

The Overvalued Asset

Imagine that your squad has a player who you believe to be overvalued. Perhaps he's a "Match of the Day player" who you suspect doesn't contribute as much as his highlights suggest. He might be a defender who makes last-ditch tackles that only give away corners, or an ageing player who is enjoying an extended run of form. Not only that, imagine that you still have a realistic chance of achieving your points or positional targets for the season.

Broadly, there are two options; reject the likely offers, or sell and replace.

1. Reject the offers: if your league objective is within reach, why create needless uncertainty? While the player's value may erode, he has clearly been a key member of the side. Football is about winning and there's a reputational cost (which varies for different clubs) to selling and then missing out on your target this season.

2. Sell and replace: given a better-than-expected return on a player, there's the opportunity to invest intelligently on a fair-value and/or younger player (notwithstanding the market reaction to your sale). There are many more unknowns here, but the benefits have the potential to be far longer-lasting than in option one.

It's a dilemma that can be resolved, at least in part, with better information. Even a back-of-the-envelope estimation of a player's points value to the team compared to a potential replacement – and the revenues associated with the possible outcomes – can give a top-level view of a player's worth.

Statistical models that indicate a player's contribution can provide another, more objective perspective. For example, our own analysis suggests that West Ham's Dimitri Payet would have been worth around 3 points to the team between December 2016 and the end of the 2016/17 season compared to a replacement-level player.

Already facing the prospect of winning less than 45 points, and despite the player being 29 years old, it took a significant offer for the money to outweigh the increased risk of relegation resulting from Payet's departure.

The point is that the strategy around a potentially overvalued player should already be established; at what price to sell (if at all), and ensuring there is a process to replace him if needed. Having a clear vision in place during the busy January period enables us to get the best from the choices we make.

Where Should We Loan Him?

Loaning out a young player comes with risk. There is no guarantee the loan will progress his development any better than staying at 'home', not to mention the uncertainties around putting him at the mercy of often unknown coaches, players and physios.

However, without some risk there is often no reward, so the question turns to finding the club that is right 'fit' for the player. This needn't be a laborious process. A simple filter, as illustrated below for an Arsenal striker like Chuba Akpom, can highlight a couple of potential destination clubs that can be approached in the first instance. This is a process that can manage the risks and give ourselves the best chance of making the experience valuable to the player's development.

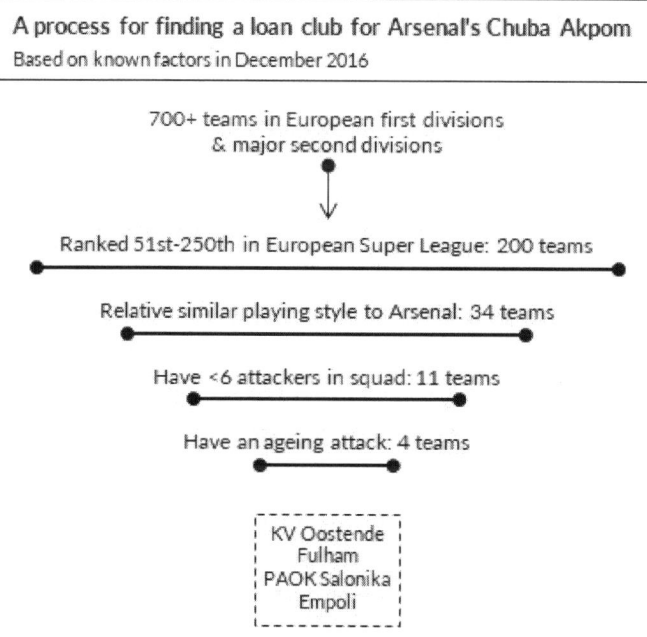

The filters go as follows:

1. Club ranked between 50th – 250th in 21st Club's European Super League: it is unlikely an elite side would

need an untested centre forward, but we may still want him playing alongside players of a reasonable standard – inside the top 250 teams in Europe.

2. Play in a relatively similar style to Arsenal: given the hope that Akpom may eventually become a first team player for Arsenal, it would be sensible to have him playing for a team that doesn't play direct or defend particularly deep.

3. Have fewer than six attackers in squad: this would help highlight teams that have relatively fewer options in attack and may be looking for greater depth.

4. Have an ageing attack: filtering for teams that have two or more attackers aged 27+ might mean these teams are looking for younger talent. What's more, the loanee may have the opportunity to learn from some more experienced heads.

The filters could of course be altered or removed – perhaps we would want to identify teams that play two up front to give a better chance of playing time, and often there are further geographical and cultural issues to consider. What's more, the filter can produce an outcome that can be mutually beneficial for both clubs in highlighting squads with potential personnel needs.

While opportunism around loan deals can occasionally strike gold, a strategic process can partially de-risk a potentially key phase in a player's development.

A Little Less Inefficient

Just as people tend to believe that the country they live in is better than most, we tend to overestimate the relative strength of our own league, and so overlook transfer targets who could improve our squad. There's a reason why players bought from strong clubs tend to be more successful at their new club. Such miscalibration bias can be described as *illusory superiority*.

And similar to how people tend to underestimate the likelihood of bad things happening, we tend to underrate the significance of a player's previous utilisation record and overestimate our ability to 'make them work' at our club. There's a reason for the correlation between a player's minutes played at the previous club and whether they play at their new club: *optimism-bias*.

And just as other industries can be biased in favour of applicants with more experience, football tends to overvalue know-how when recruiting. Yet only certain types of experience are important and so we often end up paying an unnecessary premium: *experience-bias*.

We are all biased because that's the only way to survive in a world where we have insufficient information. The problem kicks in when we allow our heuristics to affect our better judgement and ignore the information that would prevent us from making the same mistakes. Paradoxically it feels safer to follow received wisdom, even when the data suggests otherwise.

Of course there will be exceptions; the player who is able to 'step up' to a higher level, or the player who becomes a regular at their new club despite hardly getting a look in previously. But they are exceptions for a reason: they're outliers.

So then the conversation turns to one of strategy and risk. Are we prepared to take a gamble on the outliers, where both risk and reward are high? Or should we be targeting safer options, where there is a greater probability of success? Better still, can we identify the talents that others wrongly perceive to be risky, thus finding value in the market?

Irrespective of this context, with such an indifferent track record in player recruitment we must embrace every sliver of information that could help us become that little less biased and inefficient.

A Spike in Demand

The January transfer window is often a period of opportunism and seeking a short-term fix. The ability to bring players in can depend on a whole range of factors, including costs elsewhere in the squad, the seller's appetite to sell, payment terms, and so on.

The market conditions play a role too. It's useful to know how demand for certain types of players change in this different environment. Data from the English leagues in recent seasons shows that demand for attacking players increases, while demand for defensive players falls. A striker is seen as more likely to provide a quick fix than a defender.

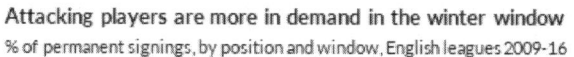

Attacking players are more in demand in the winter window
% of permanent signings, by position and window, English leagues 2009-16

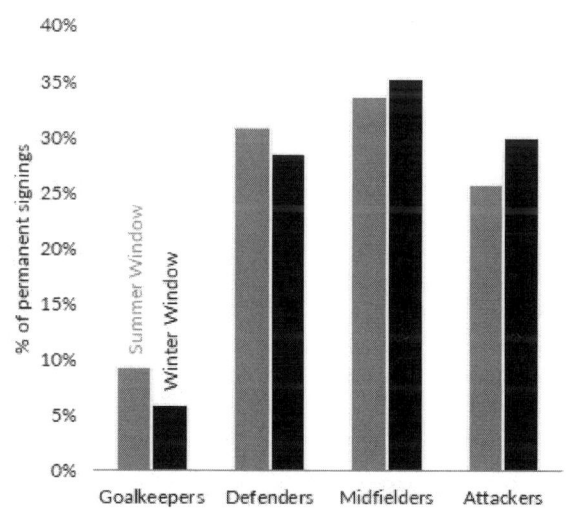

All else being equal, increased demand should be reflected in an increased price. However, the average price of a striker falls by about 15% in January (and even more so when we account for the skew of the largest transfers). What this suggests is that clubs are prepared to compromise on quality during the window because the best players simply aren't available.

For buyers, this makes the ability to execute on our preparation very important. Understanding other factors that can help secure the best deal means business can be done without being influenced by market conditions. For sellers, this knowledge can be used to move players to potentially needy clubs, obtaining a premium fee in the process.

Even if you are pressed for time towards the end of the window, there's still time to leave aside preconceptions and instead use information about the dynamics of the marketplace to your advantage.

The Endowment Effect

During any transfer window, it is worth remembering that there is a sizeable disconnect between the number of transfer rumours reported, and the number of trades that actually occur.

One simple explanation for this is that the level of evidence required to legitimately report a 'rumour' is very low. Another is that the rumours may be genuine, but that it is hard for both parties to agree on a price, causing negotiations to fail.

Such difficulty in negotiation may be explained by the endowment effect – a bias that occurs when we overvalue a good that we own, regardless of its objective market value. This essentially means that there is disparity between the price we would be willing to pay to buy something versus the price we would be willing to accept to sell the same thing. The difference between the asking price and the average offers received in the housing market is a prime example.

In football, this means we have tendency to overvalue our own player assets, often resulting in the failure of objectively fair deals, which can lead to negative outcomes for our own team. For example, failing to agree a fee for a squad player may prevent us from buying a player who would be expected to start.

To counter such bias, having a consistent and objective method to establish each player's worth to our club becomes essential. For example, understanding how many points your own players may contribute between now and the end of the season – and how this may affect your chances of promotion or your risk of relegation – can give you a tangible measure to baseline any trading assessment.

Otherwise, in the simplest terms, perhaps you could ask yourself what you would be willing to pay to acquire that player's services today?

The Right Information

In the final stages of the transfer window, where we might have three or four options to pursue, we are often faced with a deluge of information. It's the result of days, weeks, and months of information collected from scouts, analysts, and external sources like the media.

Imagine, for example, that these are some of the main facts you can remember about a potential signing as you prepare to make a decision on him:

- He is a 27-year-old centre back.

- He is from Southern Europe.

- He has experience playing for the best clubs in weaker leagues, but no experience in our league.

- He is, by all accounts, a down-to-earth character and is married with one child.

- He wins 62% of aerial contests and has a forward pass completion rate of 84%.

- He has scored five goals this season.

- He has played more than 80% of minutes in the last three seasons.

- He is in the top 20% for distance covered for centre backs.

- His agent has another client who was once a success at our club.

- His younger brother is performing well in our country in the next division down.

- Due to a lack of competition, the wages he will demand will be less than our other centre backs.

Ultimately we have to boil this information down into a prediction: will this player be a success or a failure at our club? The issue is that when held all at once, it is difficult to determine what information is a) important; b) not important; and c) missing. This is not a mental process that is easily done at the calmest of times, let alone the final week of a transfer window.

Therefore, explicit processes that red flag and weight factors to quantify the risks associated with a transfer are essential. Ongoing research can educate us about blind spots, as well alert us to other data we should collect and analyse too.

Information can be signal or noise; it helps to know which is which.

Superforecasters

If I asked you how likely your new January signing was to be a success, what would you say?

Assuming you acquired an established player, your natural instinct is that you really want your new signing to play every match between now and the end of the season to boost your chances of survival or provide fresh impetus for a charge up the table.

Before signing the player, you were probably dubious about the agent's account of why it didn't work out at the previous club, but perhaps took comfort from the coach's desire to sign him, the player's own attitude, his performance stats, and the relevant background checks. The more information you collected, the more boxes got ticked and the more optimistic you became.

Without realising, you created your own forecast of how successful your new acquisition might be. Or, more likely, how successful you wanted the acquisition to be. Because the truth is that when we really want something (or someone, in our example) to work out, we are always prone to optimism-bias.

There are a group of people, however, who would look at the problem in a different way: the 'Superforecasters'.

In fact, Superforecasters would approach the question by first asking another question of their own: how much does a typical peak-age January signing play between the close of transfer window and the end of the season?

Around 55% of minutes is the answer.

This norm (the 55%, in our example) is what statisticians call the base rate – essentially a benchmark created from past data. In our own projection conundrum, Superforecasters would start with this base rate before considering any other available information. It's worth emphasising that all the other contextual factors (the player's attitude, the background checks, his performance stats etc.) are still vital aspects of the due diligence process, it's just that Superforecasters prefer not to start there for fear of anchoring themselves in subjective waters.

In their brilliant book 'Superforecasting: The Art and Science of Prediction', co-authors Philip Tetlock and Dan Gardner suggest that we are all forecasters. *"When we think about changing jobs, getting married, buying a home, making an investment, launching a product, or retiring, we decide based on how we expect the future will fold."*

Forecasting is essentially about estimating the likelihood of something happening. The goal is not to be right every time, but rather to be less wrong most of the time. And with some healthy curiosity and a simple process grounded in objectivity, we can all be Superforecasters.

The Opportunistic Debut

During the final weeks of the European season, an increasing number of teams have fewer major placings for which to compete. With that comes an opportunity for young players to make their league debut and leave a positive impression for the following season.

It's not unfair to suggest that these opportunities can often be the result of tokenism as managers make a nod to the club's academy, but doing so in the knowledge that these matches will have little bearing on the final league table.

The problem with this opportunistic approach to youth development is clearly reflected in the data. Players who make their first start in April or May tend to make about 40% fewer starts in the following season than those who debuted between August and December.

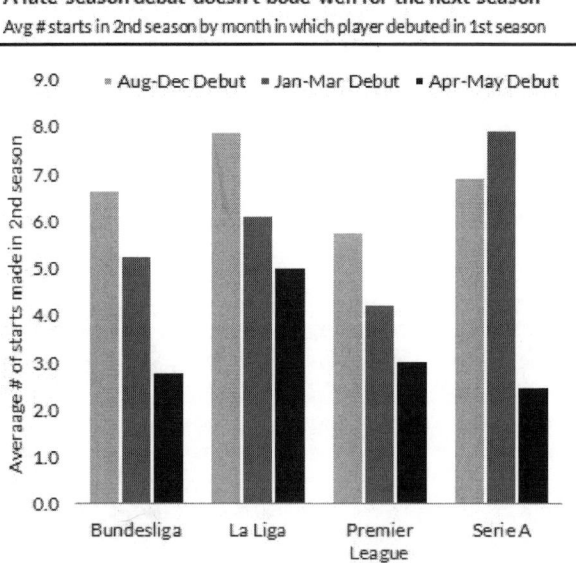

A late-season debut doesn't bode well for the next season
Avg # starts in 2nd season by month in which player debuted in 1st season

The relationship with late debuts persists into a player's third season, where those that debuted in April and May again played 40% fewer games than the early-season debutants, despite now being more than 12-18 months on from their first starts.

This isn't to say that a late-season debut directly damages a young player's prospects of becoming a first-team player, but it is more a reflection of the underlying processes that go into talent development. A debut awarded in August suggests a level of strategy and thought that has gone into the decision; the player has often demonstrated readiness in the summer and the club has made a considered decision to bring him into the first team. A debut start in April or May is more likely to be a result of league circumstance.

Southampton are an example of a club that recognises this. Since promotion back to the Premier League in 2012, all 10 youth academy players to have made a league debut start did so in January or earlier. The club's best youth prospects are always considered to be potential options at any point in the season, not just the end.

As ever, the challenge with talent development is to balance short-term risk with long-term reward. If clubs are serious about youth development, then awarding token end-of-season debuts is perhaps not the place to start

Rating Our Scouts

Player recruitment is a process that should ideally combine objectivity and subjectivity. Both aspects, however, should regularly come under suitable scrutiny and review: we should question whether we are looking at the right data, and we should question the predictions of our scouts.

While the former can require detailed statistical checks, the latter needn't be an arduous process. As key decision makers, we should have a clear view on what constitutes success from new signings. Our scouts can then provide predictions as to whether a player is likely to meet these success criteria. In due course, the predictions can be assessed against the actual outcome to give an overall score, illustrated below:

A method for checking predictions on key performance outputs			
What's the likelihood... (5 = very likely, 1 = very unlikely)	Scout Prediction	Achieved?	Points
... he starts more than 50% of matches for us?	4	Yes	+4
... he provides 8 or more assists next season?	5	No	-5
... he misses fewer than 6 matches through injury or suspenion?	4	Yes	+4
... he settles into the area and gets on well with his team mates?	3	Yes	+3
... we sell him for a positive return on investment?	2	No	-2
		Score	+4

In this case, the scout was confident on the player's ability to become a first-choice player (row 1) and provide at least 8 assists in his first season (row 2). While correct on the player's appearance record, he is penalised for overconfidence on the player's assist output, which failed to meet the success criteria standard. He is penalised less for being less confident on the player's ability to provide a return on investment (row 5), but in overall terms provided a good prediction on the player, as denoted by the +4 score.

Whether the player signs for us, or even a different club (where the scout may make a different set of predictions), this approach allows us to see who are our 'star' scouts – the people who consistently make accurate predictions about successful or unsuccessful signings.

Of course, each club will have its own unique criteria. Some clubs may detail expectations around a player's ability to his certain on-field performance outputs, while others might value off-field and commercial factors.

Whatever our priorities though, there's no reason why we shouldn't better understand the strengths and weaknesses of our scouts. Accumulating predictions over the course of a few windows should provide a useful perspective on key skills and any biases, and allow us to make the best possible decisions in the transfer market.

The Challenge of Scouting Ajax

Ajax's impressive run to the 2017 Europa League final alerted clubs across Europe to the potential of the young players in their squad, and suggested to many that they had the temperament as well as the skill to compete in bigger leagues.

While clubs have access to video as well as the ability to watch Ajax's players in person, it helps to visualise the range of possible matches any one scout could have analysed last season.

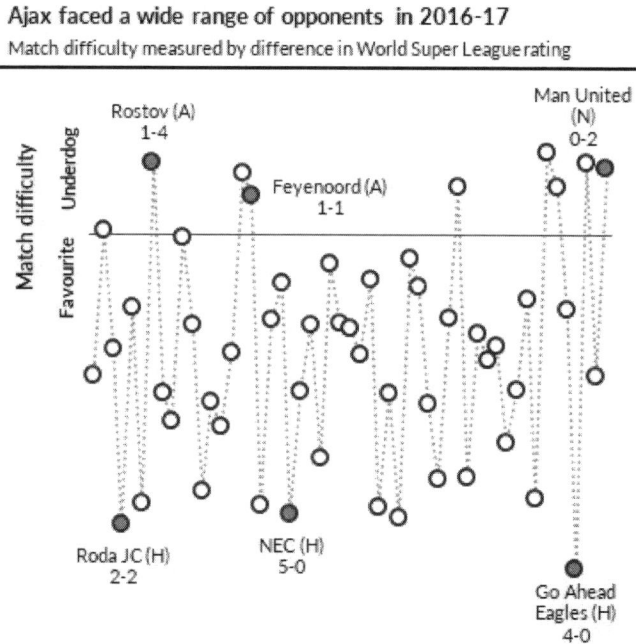

Ajax faced a wide range of opponents in 2016-17
Match difficulty measured by difference in World Super League rating

At one end, they could have seen Ajax pull off an extra time aggregate victory at Schalke, on paper the least winnable match of the season. At the other, a 4-0 win against Go Ahead Eagles was the equivalent of watching an English Premier League team play a League Two side.

This range shows the difficulty inherent in judging a player over the course of a season. It's near-impossible to watch a representative sample of performances, made harder still when certain key individuals like the head coach may only see the player once or twice.

It therefore helps to get a broader view from the data, where it is much easier to account for this variation in matches. This process should never replace the view provided by scouts, but it can remove doubts or highlight risks that may have been overlooked by only happening to watch certain games.

The challenge of scouting Ajax is indeed the challenge of scouting any team. While football is never quite "what you see is what you get", it helps to know if, at the very least, what you've seen is what he's got.

Finding Undervalued Talent

As a football industry we've been trying harder and harder in recent years to find 'undervalued talent', with mixed success.

Broadly, there are two approaches we can take. The first is bottom-up; finding traits or actions that our competitors dismiss, but actually tell us more about a player. For example, valuing the quality and quantity of chances created, rather than actual assists. Or prioritising what a player has done in his league matches rather than international tournaments.

The second approach is top-down. This is a more literal approach to finding undervalued talent – it involves looking for talented leagues and teams that pay less. Take the Czech First League, below. The latest UEFA Benchmarking Report revealed that the league's average club earned just €3.2m in 2014-15, which makes it the 29th wealthiest top division in Europe.

However, our World Super League model tells us that the clubs' performances, both domestically and internationally, mean Czech First League teams are on average the 14th-best in Europe. The average club in the Czech Republic is almost as good as an average team in the Austrian Bundesliga or Dutch Eredivisie, despite earning four and eight times less respectively.

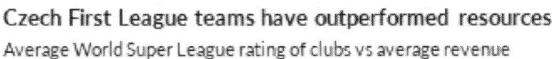

Czech First League teams have outperformed resources
Average World Super League rating of clubs vs average revenue

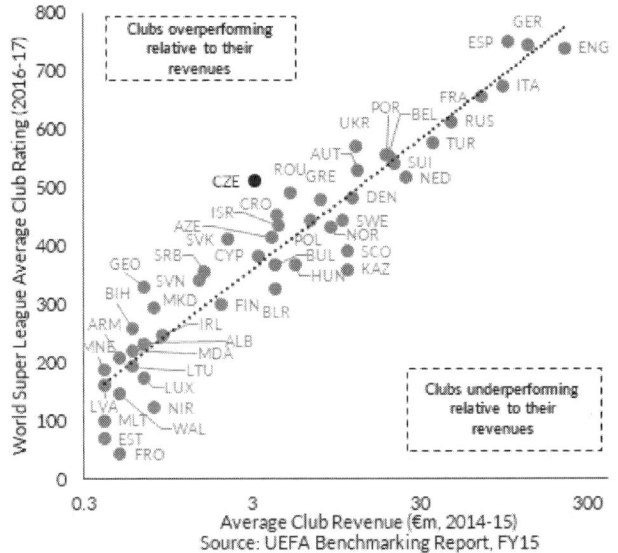

Source: UEFA Benchmarking Report, FY15

Further digging might reveal specific teams that are outperforming their resources, or it may be that Czech teams are greater than the sum of their parts (i.e. even though the teams are successful, their players are less talented). Regardless, the principles of a top-down approach are often simpler to execute. While bottom-up analysis often requires wading around in data trying to find correlations that inevitably require context, a top-down approach removes a lot of the noise and can make scouting for undervalued talent a more efficient process.

An Unwanted Record

One of the motivations behind a lot of what we do at 21st Club is the level of inefficiency in player trading. More than anything, we want to help clubs make smarter decisions with their money.

For a good example of how money is often wasted in football, we can look at club-record signings since 2010. In the 'big five' European leagues, just 56% of these signings have become 'core' players in their first season, despite commanding a fee larger than any other player in this period. That means that virtually half of all marquee signings fail to meet expectations.

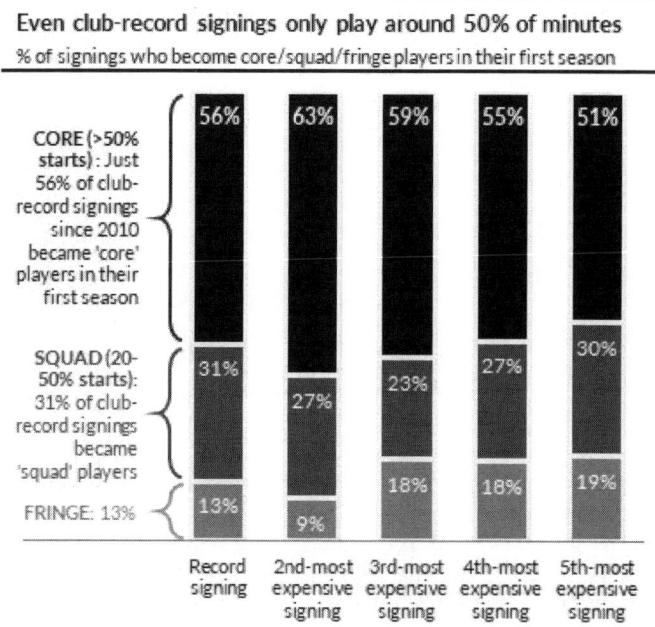

Even club-record signings only play around 50% of minutes
% of signings who become core/squad/fringe players in their first season

Curiously, the average club's second-most expensive signing since 2010 has had more success, with 63% becoming core players. But as we look at the 3rd, 4th and 5th-most expensive deals, the typical club sees these signings increasingly become squad and fringe players.

As an industry, we know we can be more prudent with our money. This doesn't mean being more frugal, it simply means having access to better and more complete information. New players come with new costs, so it's important to know – record transfers or otherwise – that the return on investment will be worthwhile.

The Realistic Recruiter

Signing new players represents one of the biggest opportunities to move the needle in football, regardless of our club's size and stature. It also carries a huge risk: the cost of getting it wrong.

Fans and other stakeholders expect new signings to make an instant impact, yet they often fail to become core players in their first season. We tend to get caught up in the noise and the urgency and seek out quick-fixes, letting the transfer window happen to us rather than by us.

The realistic recruiter thinks differently. He doesn't believe in overnight successes nor silver bullets. He first takes times to assess his own squad to identify the weakest links and possibilities for upgrades. He has a succession plan in place. He works up various scenarios and has numerous back-up options, thus maximising his negotiating buyer power. He obsesses over the details of every transfer yet thinks like a trader managing a portfolio of assets; unlikely to get it right every time, yet likely to outperform the market in the long-run with the right process.

He uses analytics to cast the net wider, while simultaneously becoming more targeted and efficient. He puts the club first, knowing that the new player is likely to be around for longer than the head coach. He uses all available information as part of his due diligence to understand potential risk and upside. He remains opportunistic, yet sticks to the plan.

The realistic recruiter mindset is available to all of us. It takes courage to challenge our existing processes and focus to ignore how the industry wants us to act. Competitive edge is often about knowing many things, rather than just one big thing.

Where to Start Your Negotiation

If you consider how much you should pay for a house, you will be influenced by the asking price. In his best-selling book *Thinking, Fast and Slow*, Daniel Kahneman tells us that the same house will appear more valuable if it's listed price is high than if it is low.

This phenomenon is known as an anchoring effect – when people consider a particular value for an unknown quantity before estimating that quantity. Even if you're determined to resist the influence of this number when making an offer for the house, research says that you're likely to stay close to the listed price, hence the image of an anchor.

The list of anchoring effect examples is endless (apparently if we're asked whether Mahatma Gandhi was more than 114 years old when he died, then we're more likely to estimate a higher number than we would if the anchoring question referred to death at 35), and so it follows that, in football, anchoring can be a powerful force in transfer negotiations.

We often convince ourselves that a player's value is based on what the market is prepared to pay, with that figure being contingent on contextual factors such as buyer and seller power. This may be true, but we also know that the market is inefficient and so understanding anchoring effects can give us an edge during negotiations.

By using intelligent, data-driven tools that are grounded in research and adjusted for world football's changing financial landscape, it is possible to get objective valuations that avoid anchoring bias.

Armed with knowledge of how market dynamics can impact the price of a footballer, those tools – such as Acquisition by 21st Club – are the best place to begin the negotiation process.

The Value of Lukaku

As an industry, one of our biggest challenges is determining value in the transfer market. Valuations are often done on gut feel, or skewed by recent deals (which in turn are often done on gut feel, and so on). We also know that having a smart starting point can have a strong impact on the final price.

The first thing to remember with valuations is that, in practice, no player has a single 'market value'. That's because any one player has vastly different values to different buying clubs – not to mention the fact that the seller has their own considerations to make.

Take Romelu Lukaku, who was sold to Manchester United from Everton for a reported £90m including add-ons. The market conditions dictated this price, but we can imagine how different circumstances might have led to a different valuation, based on changing buyer power:

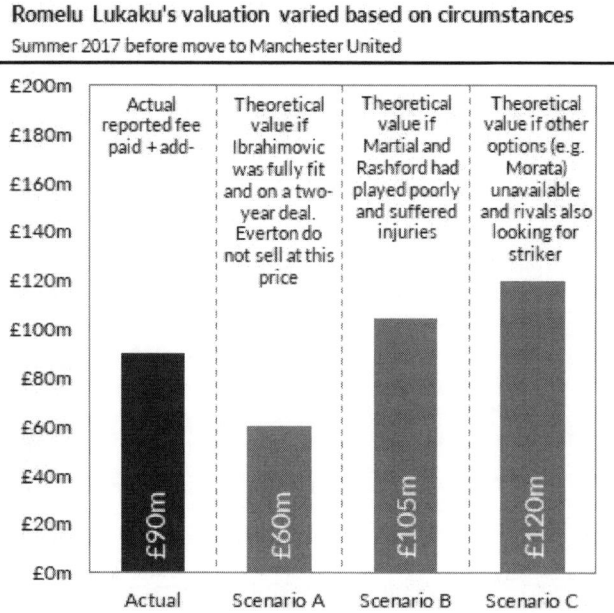

In scenario A, imagine Manchester United had given Zlatan Ibrahimovic a two-year deal in 2016, and that the Swede had performed all season without a major injury. Here, the need for Lukaku is lower, as is the upside from signing him, leading to a deflated valuation. In the absence of other buyers, perhaps Everton do not sell.

Then consider scenario B. If Manchester United's other strikers – Anthony Martial and Marcus Rashford – had underperformed in 2016/17 and suffered injuries, the impact Lukaku could have on Manchester United's performances – and therefore revenue – is much more significant.

According to our model, whereas Lukaku might earn United an extra five points a season over a fully-fit Rashford, he might earn them up to eight more than a half-fit and underperforming Rashford, as United would need to call upon other even more inexperienced options.

Finally, scenario C. Imagine three or four other Premier League teams also have a need for a top-class striker, and the supply in the market is more limited. This creates demand for elite players like Lukaku, which drives up his value – particularly when the buying clubs are rivals. This doesn't mean his value is necessarily distorted, but it may reach a stage where his price exceeds his value to Manchester United and they end up turning down the deal.

Each of these scenarios creates a very different set of outcomes. While it is impossible to account for all market conditions, a data-driven strategy can offer a more nuanced approach to player valuations and help clubs get a sense of where the market would typically be against their own valuation. Player valuations will always be some combination of art and science, but it helps to go beyond a black-and-white view and take a more considered approach.

The Point of Neymar

At the beginning of any domestic season, club's' performance expectations have been realigned based on the extent of their offseason spending.

While it is true that signings can have a significant impact on a team, the points value of a new signing is generally overstated. One of the reasons for this is that league football is a zero-sum game, meaning that to win extra points requires someone else to lose. Simply put, we just have to spend more wisely than our rivals. Secondly, one player can have a fairly limited impact on a team. Our analysis suggests that the maximum points impact of any single signing is around five, which is lower than most expect.

That low points figure is logical, though. Take Hull City and Tottenham in 2016/17 for example, with 34 and 86 points respectively. The 52-point difference means that each Tottenham player, on average, was worth just under five points compared to Hull's equivalent.

Furthermore, the impact of any new recruit is entirely relative to the player that they are replacing. Take Manchester United's signing of Romelu Lukaku. Lukaku is a fine player and, at around £75m, fair value in the market, but our player contribution model anticipates that he will have a negligible short-term impact on Manchester United's ability to win games. The reason being that he is replacing Zlatan Ibrahimovic, a player of at least equal quality and anticipated impact.

For the top teams, finding players who make a material improvement on their existing core is challenging. Even Neymar, who is undoubtedly one of the world's best, will only add around four points to PSG's expected tally in Ligue 1, assuming he replaces Ángel Di María.

So what can we take from this? Simply, that it is important to understand what the anticipated contribution of any prospective signing is. In many cases, it's perfectly legitimate to sign a player who brings limited performance upside if they maintain existing performance levels. We may have to spend just to keep pace with our rivals, as Lukaku's move and Southampton's many signings over the past few seasons bear out.

Quantifying the impact of new players in points terms will help us stay focused on the goal of winning points and ensure that we allocate our resources in the most efficient way. Ultimately, we will win more on the pitch if we are beating the market off it, and understanding player contribution is a significant step in that direction.

Everything Else Is Just Noise

Thinking clearly under pressure was one of Sir Clive Woodward's favourite mantras as coach of England's 2003 Rugby World Cup-winning side. In order to ensure his players were able to make the right calls when the heat was on, Woodward sought to recreate pressurised scenarios in training so that his team had already practiced the thought processes needed to navigate them before they took to the field.

Performing under pressure is a common theme among most high achievers, and the theatre of sport is where this is most clearly in evidence. Essentially, it boils down to making the right decision in the critical moment by processing the available information, prioritising what is important, and selecting the route most likely to deliver a favourable outcome.

The ability to think clearly is just as important in the boardroom as it is on the pitch, although the range of decisions faced and the information used varies substantially. Clarity is therefore difficult to achieve, potentially making us fall victim to cognitive biases.

Knowing which information is relevant and which sources to trust is therefore key to enabling effective and consistent decision-making in an unpredictable and inconsistent environment.

That's why we created Acquisition. Through extensive research, we know that the strength of the selling club, the player's utilisation and their age are among the key factors that determine success in recruitment. Those are the reasons we put those factors front and centre in our recruitment work, as opposed to action statistics like conversion rates, pass completion and tackles which are often assumed to be important but are substantially less correlated with success.

The idea is simple: to provide key decision-makers with information that is important, relevant and undervalued. Everything else is just noise.

High-Frequency Trading

As the dust settles after each chaotic transfer period, it's important to assess how things went during the window. While it may take some time to evaluate our new signings, it is possible to evaluate our processes: the steps that led to all the bids, negotiations and deals done.

In our own review of the summer 2017 window, one thing that struck us was that a number of players bought at the top end of the market had only been at their club for a single season.

Indeed, of the 20 most profitable single-season transfers in history, 10 were signed in the last two seasons (compared to seven of the top 20 of the all-time most expensive deals).

Most profitable transfers: player who signed in previous season
Until summer 2017

Player	Season sold	From	Via	To	Fee 1 (€m)	Fee 2 (€m)	Profit (€m)
O. Dembélé	17/18	Rennes	Dortmund	Barcelona	15	105	90
B. Mendy	17/18	Marseille	Monaco	Man City	13	58	45
D. Sánchez	17/18	Atl. Nacional	Ajax	Tottenham	5	40	35
N. Otamendi	15/16	Porto	Valencia	Man City	12	45	33
D. Drogba	04/05	Guingamp	Marseille	Chelsea	6	39	33
Á. Morata	17/18	Juventus	Real Madrid	Chelsea	30	62	32
A. Witsel	12/13	Standard	Benfica	Zenit	9	40	31
J. Rodríguez	14/15	Porto	Monaco	Real Madrid	45	75	30
A. Milik*	16/17	Leverkusen	Ajax	Napoli	3	32	29
M. Salah*	17/18	Chelsea	Roma	Liverpool	15	42	27
N. Kanté	16/17	Caen	Leicester	Chelsea	9	36	27
A. Rüdiger	17/18	Stuttgart	Roma	Chelsea	9	35	26
Marquinhos*	13/14	Corinthians	Roma	PSG	6	31	26
V. Janssen	16/17	Almere City	AZ	Tottenham	1	22	22
C. Vieri	99/00	Atlético	Lazio	Inter	28	47	18
P. Kluivert	98/99	Ajax	Milan	Barcelona	2	20	18
Dalbert	17/18	Vitória	Nice	Inter	2	20	18
A. Rahman	15/16	G. Fürth	Augsburg	Chelsea	3	20	18
F. Melo	09/10	Almería	Fiorentina	Juventus	8	25	17
G. Kondogbia	13/14	Lens	Sevilla	Monaco	4	20	16

*At profiting club for two years, with one year on loan
Reported fees, values rounded so profit may not reflect fee 2 - fee 1

Ousmane Dembélé's deal stands out – his one season in Germany earning Borussia Dortmund at least a €90m profit in fees – and took him above two players (Benjamin Mendy and Davinson Sánchez) who were signed after impressing in European competitions last season.

This evidence points to top clubs being more reactive and less strategic in the market in two key ways:

1. A lack of understanding of how players move to major leagues, which means despite enormous scouting resources they end up recruiting from other major leagues and teams.

2. A fear of missing out, as clubs look to sign players for big fees based on less evidence than before (i.e. based on one season, rather than two) in case their rivals swoop.

This activity at the top presents an opportunity for less wealthy clubs. By understanding the transfer market and using data to identify undervalued players, there's every chance a smart club can engineer a space as a middleman in the market, performing football's version of high frequency trading to earn a profit as part of its transfer strategy.

Any club can have a bad window – that's the nature of a competitive market – but there's no reason not to get our strategy and processes right.

The Football Exchange Rate

Football's global reach means the sport is unique in having many high-quality leagues dotted around the world. Therefore, unlike in the NBA or NFL (which are effectively closed leagues), understanding how performance translates across leagues is one of the single biggest challenges a club can face.

This is particularly true when looking at performance data. If a player is the most effective ball winner in Uruguay, would he sustain his output in Spain? How would a player with impressive chance creation rates in the Austrian Bundesliga expect to see his numbers change in the Italian Serie A?

Performance stats can be highly complex, so let's start with a simple one: goals. Our World Super League model enables us to create an 'exchange rate' of goals scored between leagues. Take a Danish Superliga club looking at a handful of players, all of whom have scored a goal every other game in different leagues. A player with this output in the German Bundesliga could expect to double his goals rate in the weaker Danish league, whereas an attacker stepping up from playing in Albania would see his output nearly halve.

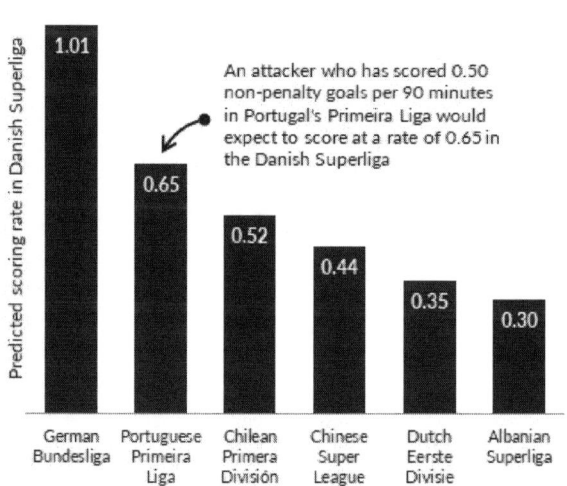

Predicted scoring rate in Danish Superliga of a 1-in-2 striker
Signing from different leagues, using the 21st Club Football Exchange Rate

An attacker who has scored 0.50 non-penalty goals per 90 minutes in Portugal's Primeira Liga would expect to score at a rate of 0.65 in the Danish Superliga

As for Chile, goals there are as valuable as they are in Denmark, a near one-to-one exchange rate. Clearly, an attacker would not be expected to score at exactly these rates, but with only anecdotes and finger-in-the-air estimates to go off, this provides a very useful starting point in translating performance numbers across leagues.

As clubs get smarter at adding context to performance data, it is important to factor in league effects. With nearly 15,000 cross-border transfers in the first nine months of this 2017 alone, smart clubs can gain an edge through calculating their football exchange rates.

The Security-Opportunity Fallacy

It's often suggested that a consequence of poor managerial job security is a lack of opportunities for young players. After all, if a head coach is fearful of losing his job, why would he take on a perceived risk?

However, the evidence suggests that this isn't the case. In the big five European leagues, managers who have been in their job longer do not tend to give more opportunities to under-23s. In some leagues, managers have actually given fewer opportunities to young players over time.

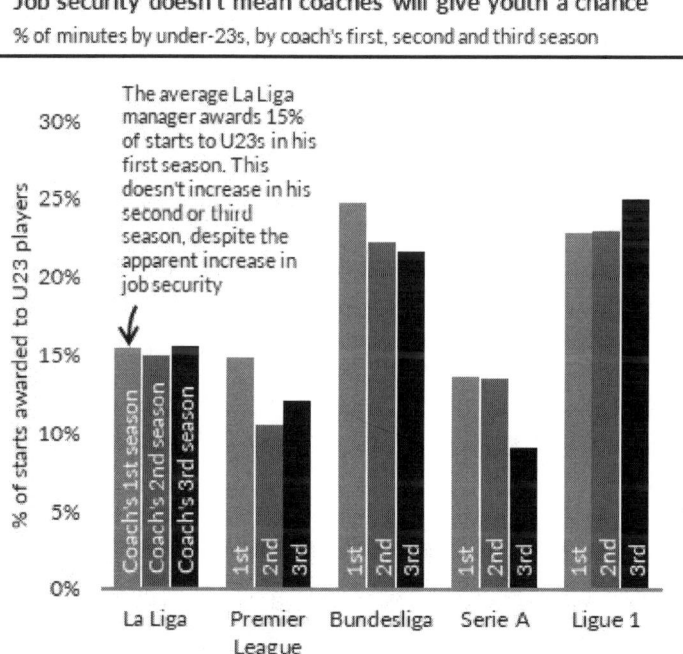

Job security doesn't mean coaches will give youth a chance
% of minutes by under-23s, by coach's first, second and third season

This suggests that a club's ability to give youth a chance is independent of their manager's security. In other words, blaming a lack of job security for a dearth of young players is just an excuse.

Smart clubs make youth development and opportunity a proactive, strategic choice. While they may hire managers who have a record of working with young players, their primary focus is to ensure that there is a long-term succession plan in place regardless of who is coaching the team.

Southampton and Feyenoord are good examples of this; even as managers have been replaced or poached, the practice of giving youth a chance has been unchanged.

In youth development, security doesn't equal opportunity; strategy does.

What's The Worst That Can Happen?

Risk is one of the many excuses for failing to grant first team opportunities to young players. With so much at stake, coaches often prefer the perceived reliability of experience at the expense of blocking the talent pathway. With the average managerial tenure hovering a little over 12 months, coaches are naturally inclined to focus on the short term at the expense of granting opportunities to young prospects.

There are two things here. The first is the misconception that playing youth players is a material risk. The data suggests that when teams have given greater opportunities to youth players, the impact on results has been negligible on average. In other words, giving youth a chance is not correlated – positively or negatively – with success. Reducing the perception of risk is one way to unblock the pathway to the first team.

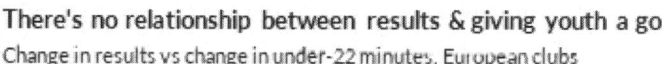

There's no relationship between results & giving youth a go
Change in results vs change in under-22 minutes, European clubs

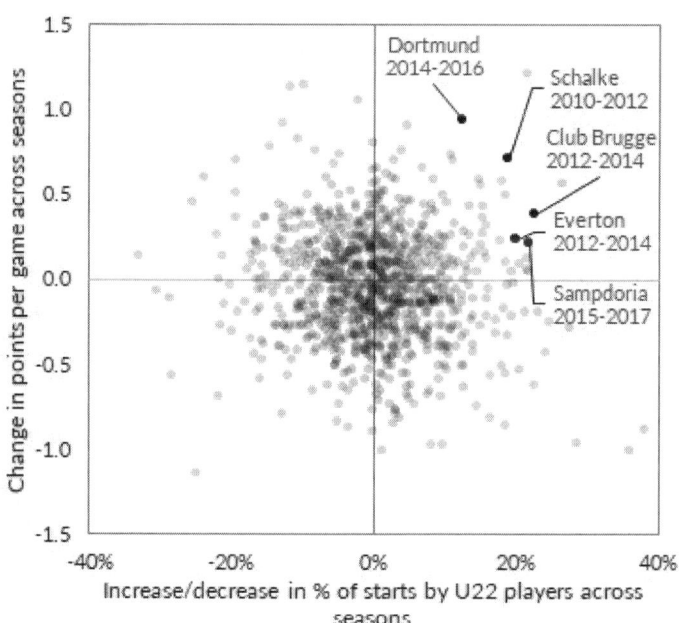

The second point is around impetus. Clubs that successfully create an environment where coaches are either empowered, encouraged or forced to give the kids a chance are well-placed to successfully develop their own future stars. This doesn't mean that you can simply play any young player at any time, but by taking a strategic approach to creating opportunity we can give ourselves a better chance of success. This may be through cultural change, positive incentives that reward coaches for playing young players, or enforced restrictions, such as limiting squad sizes.

Schalke in 2010/11 (highlighted above) were a team that successfully integrated youth players into the first team. Players like Julian Draxler, Joel Matip, Lewis Holtby and Kyriakos Papadopoulos helped the club climb from 14th in the Bundesliga in 2010/11 to 3rd in 2011/12. That is not to say that those players were the reason for climbing the table – there were likely a number of factors at play – but playing them certainly didn't hinder Schalke's performance.

With the relative cost of developed rather than acquired talent, the rewards are there for clubs who have young talent and the impetus to grant them an opportunity.

Selling Our Coutinho

Selling our best player is an immensely difficult decision. We are naturally loss averse and want to protect what we have. We imagine all the things that could go wrong without them. This is even harder in January, when it is felt the disruption is magnified.

Key decision makers at Liverpool probably went through this process in January 2018. Philippe Coutinho seemed to make the team tick, and there was a sense that his departure could have derailed Liverpool's season entirely.

One way to fight these feelings is to look at the evidence. If we look historically at clubs who had a high net income in the January window (that is, they sold valuable player(s) without bringing expensive talent in), many saw performance deteriorate. However, the deterioration was much less than many would assume. After accounting for fixtures and the role of luck, the biggest drops in performance were less than 0.1 points per game. Over half a season, that's less than two points.

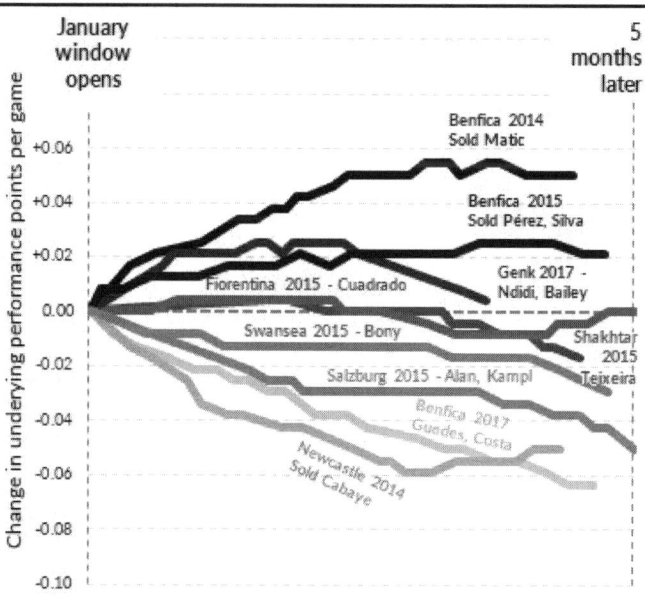

Selling a star in winter has cost less than 0.1 points per game
Clubs with high net income in January window & impact on performance

In some cases, a potential drop of two points is significant enough to deter us from doing a deal, no matter how lucrative. Nevertheless, it is smaller than we sometimes fear, partly because we often underestimate the quality of our replacement-level player – something we measure with our Player Contribution model. In the case of Coutinho, where we estimate a similar cost in performance versus replacement, £142m far outweighs the potential loss of a Champions League place.

That isn't to say results can't fall off a cliff after the sale of a star player, but to attribute it to the sale alone would be overly reductive. Indeed, some teams can even kick on and improve; Benfica have made a habit of this.

Ultimately, strategic clubs try to estimate, in objective, considered terms, the on-field impact of a player and weigh it up against the offer received. Often we'll find that the offer is too good to refuse.

Apples to Apples

The European Golden Boot is an annual award recognising the best goalscorer in European club football. It was initially awarded every season to the player who scored the most goals in European first divisions. The early winners were a mix of household names, such as Marco van Basten, and relative unknowns, like Cypriot Sotiris Kaiafas. In 1991, the award was cancelled due to controversy over a Cypriot player missing out on the award despite scoring more goals than the actual winner.

The central issue, of course, was that the level of play varied widely across different leagues. It was much easier to score against defences in the Cypriot first division than against those in England or Italy. The award was restarted in 1997, this time making use of UEFA country coefficients. According to the coefficients, goals scored in the top five European leagues are worth more than those scored in lower-ranked leagues. This brought the winners more in line with what people would intuitively expect. Since the 2009/10 season, the only winners have been Lionel Messi, Cristiano Ronaldo, and Luis Suárez.

The lesson is that when we want to compare apples to apples, we need to keep the nature of measurements in mind and make the necessary adjustments. The initial award wanted to avoid statistics altogether and ended up providing answers that were clear and simple, but wrong.

This is why we developed the 21st Club Football Exchange Rate. We want to provide the most accurate adjustments possible, so that when we're recruiting a striker who has scored 20 goals in a different league, we can understand how many goals that would translate to in our own league.

The 2016-17 European Golden Shoe - using the Football Exchange Rate

	European Golden Shoe 2016/17 Season					Using the Football Exchange Rate Adjusting for possible minutes & penalty goals				
	Name	Lge.	Goals	Factor	Pts	Name	Lge.	Goals	Exchange Rate to B'liga*	Pts
1	Messi	ESP	37	2	74	Messi	ESP	37	1.00	37.0
2	Dost	POR	34	2	68	Aubameyang	GER	31	1.00	31.0
3	Aubameyang	GER	31	2	62	Lewandowski	GER	30	1.00	30.0
4	Lewandowski	GER	30	2	60	Suárez	ESP	29	1.00	29.0
5	Suárez	ESP	29	2	58	Kane	ENG	29	1.00	28.9
6	Džeko	ITA	29	2	58	Cavani	FRA	35	0.75	26.4
7	Kane	ENG	29	2	58	Modeste	GER	25	1.00	25.0
8	Mertens	ITA	28	2	56	Ronaldo	ESP	25	1.00	25.0
9	Cavani	FRA	35	1.5	52.5	Lukaku	ENG	25	1.00	24.9
10	Belotti	ITA	26	2	52	Džeko	ITA	29	0.84	24.3
11	Lukaku	ENG	25	2	50	Sánchez	ENG	24	1.00	23.9
12	Modeste	GER	25	2	50	Mertens	ITA	28	0.84	23.4
13	Ronaldo	ESP	25	2	50	Dost	POR	34	0.68	23.2
14	Higuaín	ITA	24	2	48	Belotti	ITA	26	0.84	21.8
15	Sánchez	ENG	24	2	48	Lacazette	FRA	28	0.75	21.1
16	Icardi	ITA	24	2	48	Werner	GER	21	1.00	21.0
17	Immobile	ITA	23	2	46	Higuain	ITA	24	0.84	20.1
18	Lacazette	FRA	28	1.5	42	Icardi	ITA	24	0.84	20.1
19	Werner	GER	21	2	42	Costa	ENG	20	1.00	19.9
20	Costa	ENG	20	2	40	Agüero	ENG	20	1.00	19.9
21	Agüero	ENG	20	2	40	Immobile	ITA	23	0.84	19.3
22	Aspas	ESP	19	2	38	Aspas	ESP	19	1.00	19.0
23	Berg	GRE	24	1.5	36	Alli	ENG	18	1.00	17.9
24	Alli	ENG	18	2	36	Terodde	GER (2)	25	0.71	17.7
25	Insigne	ITA	18	2	36	Smolov	RUS	18	0.94	17.0

*The Bundesliga is the 'base' league to exchange to, accounting for the fact that it has just 34 games

Take Simon Terodde for example, who scored 25 goals for Stuttgart in the Bundesliga 2 in 2016/17. Our best estimate for the exchange rate to the Premier League, taking into account both the quality of the league and the number of games played in a season is 0.71. That means a player who scored 25 goals in a Bundesliga 2 season would be expected to score 17 or 18 goals in a Premier League or Bundesliga season. Without such a method of conversion it would be all too easy to write off Terodde's form and overlook him simply because he was playing in a second tier division.

Bill James once said that the alternative to good statistics is not "no statistics," it's "bad statistics." If we try to avoid statistics and make no adjustments, we will inevitably end up comparing apples to oranges along the way and reach wrong conclusions. However, using statistics it is certainly possible to compare apples to apples and get an accurate idea of goalscoring capability across very different leagues.

III: PERFORMANCE

The Early Indicators

During the opening weeks of the season it is desperately difficult to gauge the state of affairs. Not only are new players settling in, the skew of the fixture calendar can make some teams appear better or worse than they are.

We can use two composite metrics to give us an early sense of how well our team is currently performing and will likely continue to perform over the coming weeks. The first is results compared to performance; have we deserved the points we've won? The second is performance compared to pre-match expectations; have we performed better than we reasonably could have expected based on the difficulty of matches? These metrics are plotted for La Liga teams as they stood in September 2016 on the horizontal and vertical axis respectively.

Early season: tracking results, performance and expectations
La Liga 2016-17, after seven matches

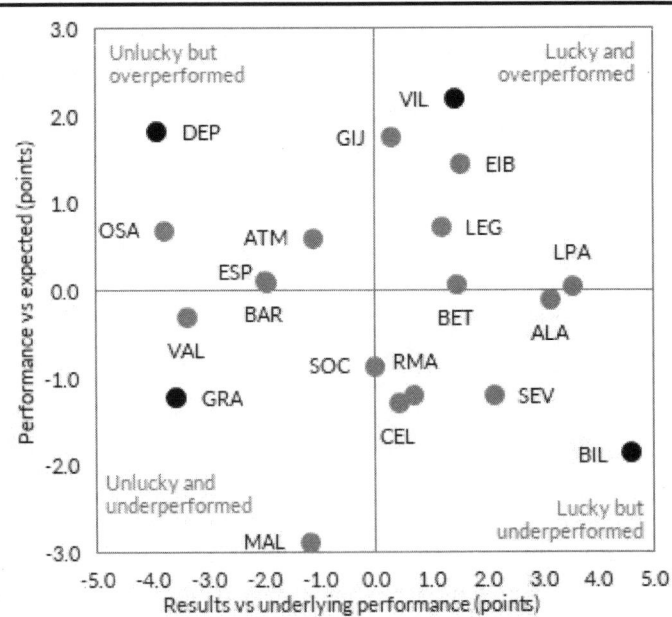

Let's look at some of the extreme examples:

Deportivo La Coruña may have sat third-bottom, but they could consider themselves unlucky, having deserved about four more points than the five they had accumulated at that stage. What's more, they'd performed well against some tough opponents, so could take a lot of positives despite their league position.

Villarreal had gotten fractionally more than they'd deserved, but had still performed admirably given their fixtures.

Athletic Bilbao may have had points on the board, but a couple of slightly fortuitous victories meant they could be considered a little lucky to have been fifth. What's more, their performances hadn't been up to what might have been expected of them.

Granada perhaps deserved a little more from their matches up to that point, but there was no getting away from the fact they'd underperformed, particularly in their latest two games. The season was shaping up to be a struggle.

While results are ultimately the only thing that produces tangible reward in May, some contextualised metrics can give a better, more predictive picture of where we really are today.

How to Win On Saturday

When we refer to 'strategy' in football, we normally think of processes where the results may not materialise for months or even years. A club's strategy might seek to exploit inefficiencies in the transfer market or youth development, for example.

A football club boardroom can however also focus on strategies that will help the team win on the weekend. Specifically, there are three notable in-game inefficiencies that can be exploited with better strategy, processes and hires:

Home advantage: initial 21st Club research suggests that the crowd forms as much as a third of home field advantage, with familiarity, travel and other factors comprising the rest. Knowing how to maximise these factors can lead to better results both at home and on the road.

Game states: teams are less effective when they're winning; after controlling for the strength of teams and venue, we find that the losing team is about 20-25% more likely to score the next goal than the leading team. Knowing how to fight loss aversion can make a substantial difference to results.

Set pieces: there is no relationship between open play team ability and set piece ability (below), which presents an enormous opportunity for weaker teams to punch above their weight on a weekly basis.

Poor teams from open play can be good at set pieces

Open play performance vs set piece performance, big 5 leagues 2015-16

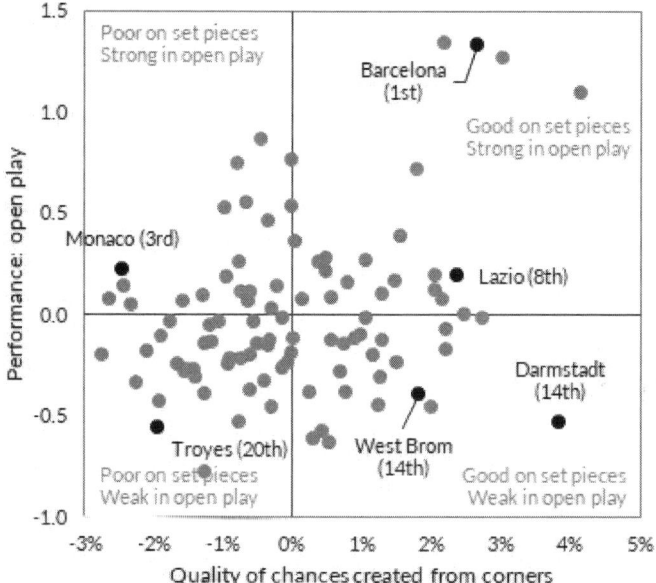

While we are often swept up in the noise of week-to-week results, there's no reason not to take a strategic view of the things that can make a difference every weekend.

Controlling The Uncontrollable

It is an inarguable fact that we can win or lose football matches due to factors that are outside of our control. We exert significant influence on results through team selection, motivation and sound coaching, but on any given day we can only leave marginal penalty calls, the opposition keeper's performance and that of our own forwards to chance.

Over a season, how our cards fall can leave us finishing higher or lower in the table than we would expect based on the relative quality of our team. Simply put, these uncontrollable factors cause variance.

The principal reason why variance exists is that football is a low-scoring sport – a goal is more influential on the outcome of a match than, say, a three-pointer in basketball or a penalty in rugby. Teams often lose games that they really deserved to win based on performance alone. In fact, our analysis suggests that, on average, the better team (that is the team that creates notably more dangerous chances) wins only around 64% of the time.

While the factors that cause variance may be outside of our control, the extent to which we are affected by them is not. The premise is simple: variance is the result of football's low scoring nature, so it can be reduced by making the games higher scoring.

The data bears this out – our analysis suggests that the better team wins around 75% of the time in games with over 2.5 goals vs. 50% in games with fewer than 2.5 goals.

This means that we can dictate the extent to which our results reflect our quality. So the best team in the league should want to play in high scoring matches to limit the chances of an upset while the weakest team should do the opposite by seeking to limit scoring opportunities. Bayern Munich in the Bundesliga and Pisa in Serie B, whose matches up to the February of the 2016/17 season involved an average of 2.9 and 1.0 goals respectively, are good examples of these two extremes.

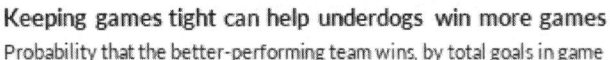

Keeping games tight can help underdogs win more games
Probability that the better-performing team wins, by total goals in game

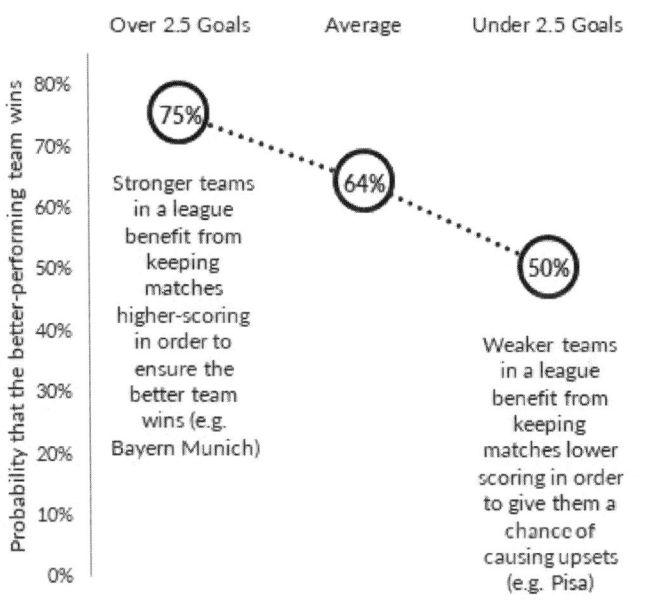

This is interesting for clubs who span two competitions of differing opponent strengths. Domestically, Celtic adopt an open approach to limit the opportunity for upset, with their matches averaging around 3.1 goals since 2013. This serves them well in the Scottish Premiership where they are comfortably the strongest team, but when out-gunned on paper, as they often are in the Champions League, they struggle to compete. During each season of the same period of domestic dominance, Celtic have either failed to qualify for the Champions League at all or failed to emerge from their group.

Celtic's context is distinct, but we can take much from their example. Are we a club that needs to take a chance on variance, or are we better served by trying to get no more or less than we deserve? To answer this, we need to clearly understand our own context, aspirations and appetite for risk, but even asking the question will help us begin to take greater control.

The Impact Manager

We know from our research that, on average, managerial changes make little difference to the performance of a team in the long run. That isn't to say, however, that smart hires can't turn struggling teams around.

When we look through our database of managers who did improve performance in their first 20 matches in charge, one thing stands out: the biggest improvements tended to be in defence rather than in attack.

New head coaches tend to make bigger impacts in defence
Change in attack/defence team rating in first 20 games under new coach

The biggest improvements in defence were worth about 6-10 points to the team over a season, whereas the biggest improvements in attack were worth around 4-6 points.

This is in line with most people's intuition; a club in crisis often needs better defensive organisation, something that can be coached over a relatively short period of time. Attacking performance, however, is much more reliant on the individual talent at a manager's disposal, and therefore more likely to be improved via promotions from the academy or through player trading.

This has implications for our approach to both manager and player recruitment. Clubs that desire an attacking, free-flowing style of football need to either be patient with a new head coach as he tries to change things with existing resources, or be prepared to spend in order to improve the squad's attacking output.

This of course should also be done in the context of whether being a good defensive team or a good attacking team gives us a better chance of reaching our targets. New managers can make a strong, positive impact, but expectations need to be aligned with the reality of what can and is likely to be achieved.

On Protecting That Lead

Pep Guardiola said that his failure to convince his Manchester City players to attack in Monaco during their 2016/17 Champions League last 16 tie was the reason for their elimination. "I tried to convince them in all the meetings we had to come here, try to attack and score," said Guardiola. "My mistake was being not able to convince them to do that."

In the context of the tie, City were 5-3 ahead after the first leg at the Etihad Stadium. Guardiola's post-match comments suggested that he was all too aware of the perils in trying to protect a lead.

We see this in football all the time. When a team goes ahead, they often sit back and try to defend their winning position. The problem is, they don't tend to do it very well: our analysis shows that teams concede goals at a higher rate per minute when leading in matches than when level or behind. As a result, teams relinquish leads more often than we would expect.

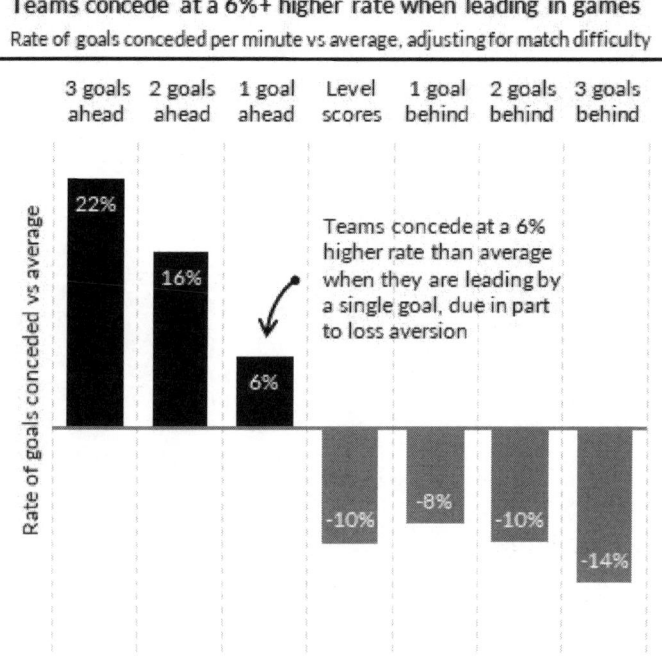

Teams concede at a 6%+ higher rate when leading in games
Rate of goals conceded per minute vs average, adjusting for match difficulty

Our tendency to prefer avoiding losses to acquiring equivalent gains – loss aversion – is prevalent in all walks of life and leads to risk aversion. For example, a risk-averse investor might stay away from adding high-risk stocks or investments to their portfolios (and often lose out on higher rates of return). Similarly, a golfer may avoid the possibility of loss by playing more conservatively when they have the opportunity to make a birdie, yet will be more aggressive if they are at risk of a bogie (costing the golfer shots and reducing their earnings potential). Psychologically it hurts more to lose something.

So, is there anything we can do to get past our aversion to loss?

The natural tendency is to throw money at the problem – "what if we were to incentivise the players (and the head coach) to keep attacking, even when the team are already ahead?" Yet you have to wonder whether – in the heat of battle – top players are really thinking about money, especially when their earnings are already relatively high and their will to win (by trying to protect their lead) so strong.

So how about non-financial means? Apparently, when at Manchester United, Rene Meulensteen developed an end-of-training game whereby competing teams would each draw a playing card from a randomly shuffled deck, and the card number would dictate how many goals each team needed to score to win. Not knowing your opponent's hand forced each team to keep attacking, irrespective of whether they were already ahead.

Loss aversion is deeply ingrained in our psyches, hence why Guardiola found it tough to "convince" his players to keep attacking against Monaco. Changing this mindset is easier said than done, yet the team who finds a way will have uncovered another small edge on the road to overachievement.

The Undeserving Champion

"We need in football this type of luck," said Liverpool manager Jürgen Klopp of Emre Can's improbable goal against Watford in May 2017. A loss for Liverpool would have cut their chances of a top four finish to 62%; a little more than a coin flip. As it was, Liverpool's win gave them a 90% chance of playing Champions League football next season.

The dramatic swing in Liverpool's fortunes illustrates the fine margins that exist at the end of the season, and, by extension, the absurdity of the belief that every team gets what they deserve. For it can't be said that just because Can pulled off an unlikely strike, Liverpool deserved their place in the top four, just as it can't be said that Liverpool would have been less deserving of their place had he missed.

The reality is that luck – whether it is unsustainable streaks, refereeing decisions, or simply moments that happen to transpire in a convenient way (like Can's goal, as Klopp put it) – doesn't 'even out' as we might like it to. Clubs accumulate deficits and credits that push them into league positions they don't deserve. Like a gambler who loses on a few spins, there is no universal force to give him what he is 'due'.

The sooner we accept this, the sooner we can critically assess our season. The odds are we probably haven't got what we've deserved, so it's time to identify those critical moments that could have gone another way and objectively assess where we really are as a team.

The Biggest Bang for Your Buck

Finding the balance between what we want and what we can afford is a key part of player recruitment. Often our grandiose summer plans are left unfulfilled by the time the new season arrives, with necessary compromise having thwarted our ambitions.

But there are some simple things that we can do to maximise the performance returns of our investment. For example, investing in our defense, while unglamorous, can yield a much greater performance return than seeking out expensive, attacking recruits.

Let's take a look at four of the strongest teams in the Europe according to our World Super League (WSL) as it stood in May 2017. In terms of overall strength, there is very little separating Barcelona, Real Madrid, Atlético Madrid and Juventus.

If we look at how our model rates each team in terms of attack and defense, two distinctive approaches to team building become evident. On the one hand, Barcelona and Real are predominantly attacking forces filled with expensively acquired attacking gems, while Juve and Atlético are more defensively impressive, with a greater focus on organisation over flair.

However, this only becomes relevant to our recruitment plans when we consider the relative market value of each team. Barcelona and Real's value relative to that of Atlético and Juve shows which of the approaches costs the most to execute.

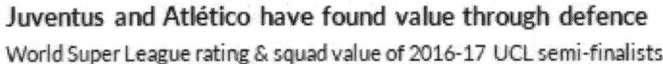

Juventus and Atlético have found value through defence

World Super League rating & squad value of 2016-17 UCL semi-finalists

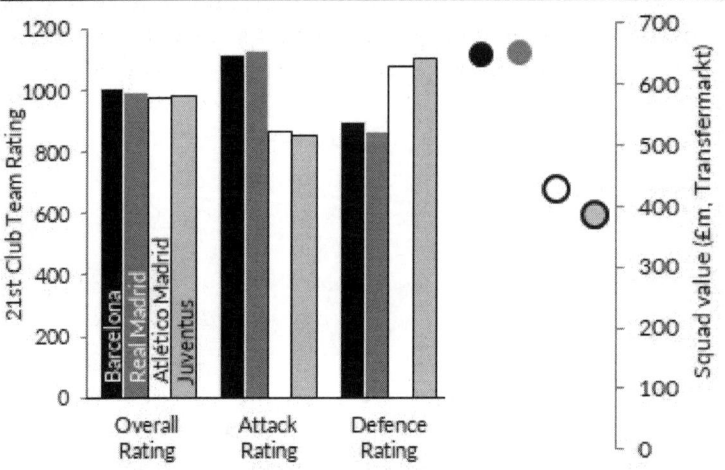

So what can we take from this?

Simply put, acquiring defensive talent is cheaper and doesn't necessarily impinge on our ability to be a good team. For financially stretched teams, therefore, investing in your defense may yield the biggest return in performance terms. Clearly there is a balance to be struck – Pisa had the second best defensive record in Serie B but still finished at the foot of the table – and many other factors to consider, but where resources are limited and the attack is at least fit for purpose, buying for the back might yield the biggest bang for your buck.

Got, Expected, Deserved, Need

During the early stages of the season, when the league table often lies, it can be easy to over- or underreact to results. As such, it helps to have some objective information on how the season has and might progress.

We recommend focusing on four key metrics:

- How many points have we got? (Points per game)

- How many points were we objectively expected to get pre-match? (Expected points per game)

- How many points did we deserve to get based on our performance? (Performance points per game)

- How many points do we need to get to achieve our target? (Required points per game)

Take the teams in the English Championship below, where this information can help get a gauge on their respective seasons to date.

Four metrics that can help evaluate early-season form
Championship clubs after four matches, 2017-18 season

Club	Got	Expected	Deserved	Assumed Target	Need	Summary
Ipswich Town	3.0	1.4	1.0	Safety	0.9	Despite good start, form likely to turn
Nottingham Forest	2.3	1.3	1.3	Top Half	1.2	Results unsustainable, but top half still likely
Aston Villa	1.0	1.2	1.5	Top 2	1.9	Improvements required for top 2 push
Millwall	0.5	1.1	2.0	Safety	1.1	Performances suggest safety still possible
Brentford	0.3	1.6	1.7	Top 6	1.7	Performances suggest top 6 still possible

For example, four points from four games ('got') was fewer than Aston Villa would have objectively 'expected' going into the 2017/18 campaign. While performances ('deserved') exceeded that expectation, it was still below the 'need' requirement of 1.9 points per game from there on out to finish in the top two. In other words: the team had been unlucky, but the board should keep track of performance as a leading indicator to see whether changes are needed later in the season to get up to the 'need' threshold.

These metrics help to reassure clubs like Millwall and Brentford that performance levels are on or even above target despite results. For Ipswich and Nottingham Forest, they temper expectations but show how good early-season results created a cushion.

It may be early days, but when making the big decisions – whether to sign a player or change the head coach – smart boardrooms take the emotion out of the room and stay on top of the metrics that matter.

A Temperature Check

If you wanted to go somewhere warm on holiday, which city would you choose: New York or Sydney?

While Sydney is six degrees hotter on average over a year, no one would buy flights to Australia on this information alone. New York City is warmer from May to September, and Sydney warmer for the rest of the year – that much is obvious.

In football, if we're asked whether Team A is better than Team B, we invariably look at the league table for an answer. The problem is that for many leagues this average is fixed between August and May, and therefore disguises the variation in 'temperatures' for each team.

Tottenham Hotspur have been particular victims of this. They won fewer points than Leicester City in the period between August 2015 and May 2016, fewer than Chelsea between August 2016 and May 2017, and fewer than Manchester City between August and November 2017. In other words, they've won fewer points than three other teams in three distinct August to May (or November) periods.

If you dig a bit deeper though, Spurs were the 'hottest' team in England for parts of the last 30 months. Rather than just judging seasons as ending in May, Spurs had won more points over 38 games than any other team in England at multiple points last season. While fixture balance may have played a part in this, our World Super League model estimates that they were actually the best team in the country for an even more significant part of last season, and have been the country's best team in the calendar year of 2017.

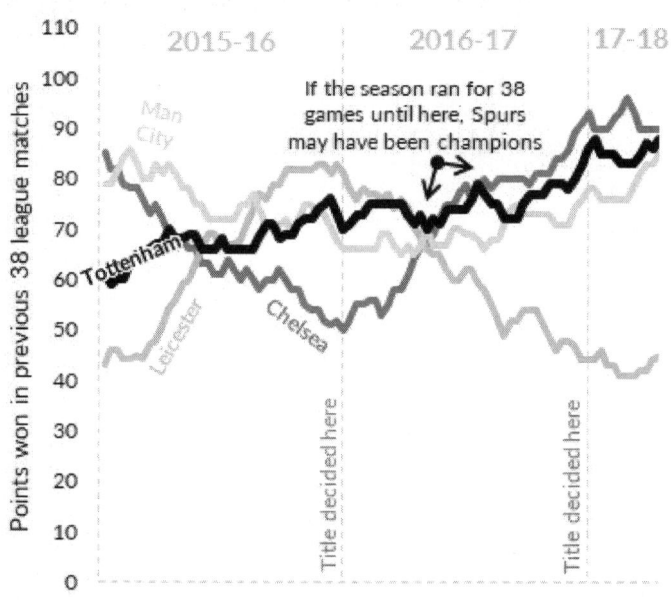

Spurs have topped the last-38 table at the wrong time
38-match rolling total of points, selected Premier League teams to Nov '17

If the season ran for 38 games until here, Spurs may have been champions

It's fair to ask why this matters – after all, it's the final league table that determines who is champions and who is relegated. However, we also make a lot of decisions based on the league table that is printed in newspapers every week. We decide who to buy, who to sell, whether to change the manager, promote a young player, and so on. Many clubs in Spurs' position might have decided they needed more leaders in the squad because they had fallen short in May twice, when really it was just that the calendar hadn't quite aligned for the team. We just took their temperature at the wrong time.

Sophisticated tools like our World Super League – or even a simple perspective like the one above – can help us plan that little bit better than clubs that are slaves to the league table.

More That What We Paid For

In November 2017, Sporting Intelligence released their annual Global Sports Salaries Survey (GSSS), providing insight into how pay varies across top sports leagues.

The inclusion of average first team pay in the big five European leagues means that, using our World Super League (which ranks teams globally according to how good they are), we can compare teams on a like-for-like basis and assess which clubs are getting the biggest bang for their buck.

While we often think of small-budget teams overachieving, the three biggest overachievers versus pay were Atlético Madrid, Tottenham Hotspur and Barcelona, with Getafe and Atalanta – who are in some cases as good as teams paying four times as much – not far behind. For some, wealth has not given way to complacency.

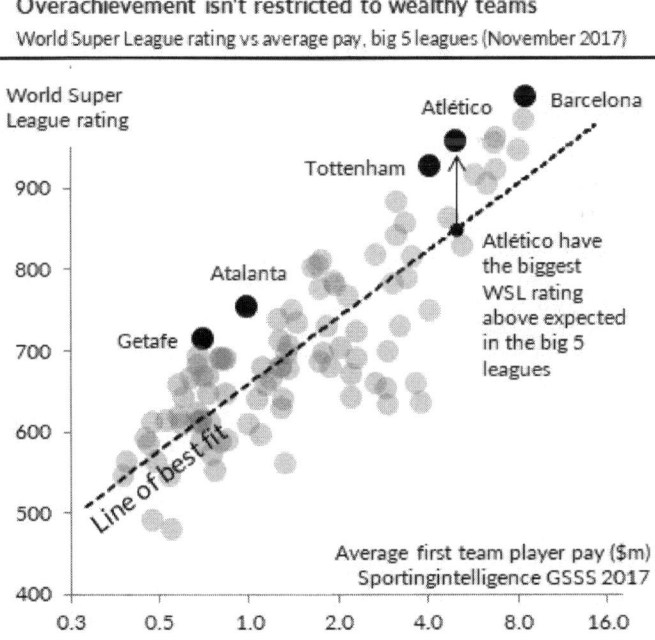

The relative efficiency of these clubs is notable in part due to the inefficiency of many (and often, but not exclusively English) mid-budget teams, highlighting how sport is a zero-sum industry.

For the overachievers, there may be challenges when their players argue they deserve greater pay for their performance, provided this isn't covered in variable pay. For everyone else though, they serve as role models, because regardless of their budget they have been able to overachieve due to factors including youth development (e.g. Atalanta), to recruitment and coaching (e.g. Atlético), and to a clear club philosophy (e.g. Barcelona).

The imperfect relationship between wins and pay means there are inefficiencies to exploit, regardless of how much we have to pay our players.

The Money League Trend

The 21st annual Deloitte Money League report, published in January 2018, highlighted the rate of financial growth at the top of the game, with revenues up 6% in the top 20 and as much as 58% for Leicester City and 46% for Internazionale.

Combined with our own World Super League, which ranks teams globally in one 'league table' based on performance, the DML again highlights that while wealth enables clubs to reach a certain level, sustained high performance comes through finding competitive edge.

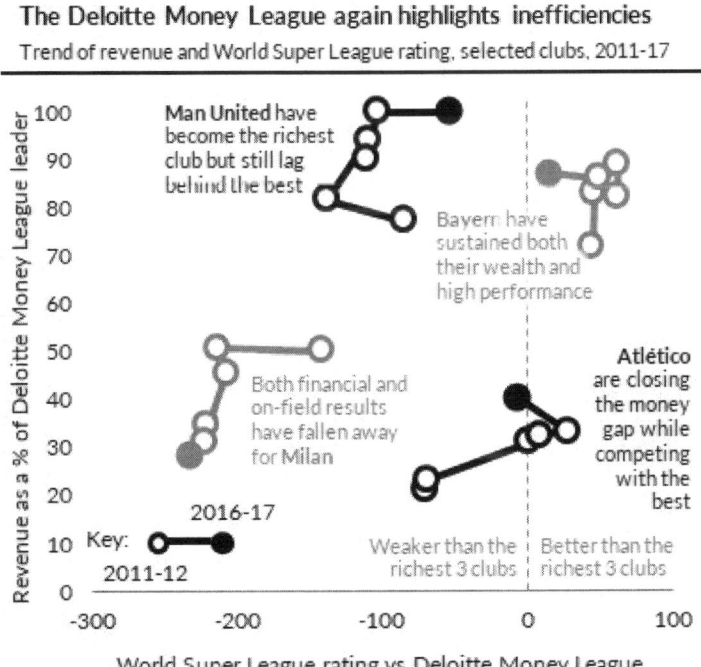

The Deloitte Money League again highlights inefficiencies

Trend of revenue and World Super League rating, selected clubs, 2011-17

Man United have become the richest club but still lag behind the best

Bayern have sustained both their wealth and high performance

Both financial and on-field results have fallen away for Milan

Atlético are closing the money gap while competing with the best

Key: 2016-17 / 2011-12

Weaker than the richest 3 clubs | Better than the richest 3 clubs

World Super League rating vs Deloitte Money League top 3 average

Milan, for example, are an ever-present in the DML top 30, but the club now ranks 50th in our World Super League. Decline in on-field performance has precipitated a drop out of the Money League top 10 (in 2014) and then top 20 (2017), as rivals have seemingly caught up with their innovations in areas such as sports science, for example.

Atlético Madrid, meanwhile, found an edge through succession planning, recruitment and playing style, and are slowly closing the financial gap in the process. Manchester United too have closed a financial gap – such that they have topped the DML for the last two years – but are yet to outperform their equally-wealthy rivals on the pitch.

There's no denying that on a global scale financial muscle brings results, but as many as 10 teams in our World Super League top 30 are not in Deloitte's list this year. Smart clubs place value on being in this group of overachievers.

It Never Evens Out

We're often told that luck will even out over a season. After all, a year is a long time, and it seems absurd that one team would repeatedly have things go their way or against them.

However, this misunderstands the true nature of 'luck'. True luck, or randomness, is blind to what happened before, and can go either way in the future. The fact that a team might have had a few games where they were 'unlucky' – perhaps they've repeatedly been denied by unusually good goalkeeping, or have seen their opponents score multiple low-probability attempts – doesn't mean they will enjoy some good luck in the future, that they are 'due' some good fortune. That run could continue well past the length of a season.

One way to visualise this is to look at the FA Cup. In each round until the semi-finals, clubs have a 50/50 chance of getting drawn to play at home, which is clearly preferable. Of the current 'big six' clubs, some – like Chelsea, Manchester United and Tottenham Hotspur – have been lucky in this respect, getting far more home ties than away, while others – particularly Manchester City, but also Liverpool – have been unlucky. Even after 250+ cup draws and over 100 years of matches, there isn't a universal force that 'evens out' the luck.

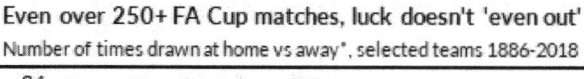

Even over 250+ FA Cup matches, luck doesn't 'even out'
Number of times drawn at home vs away*, selected teams 1886-2018

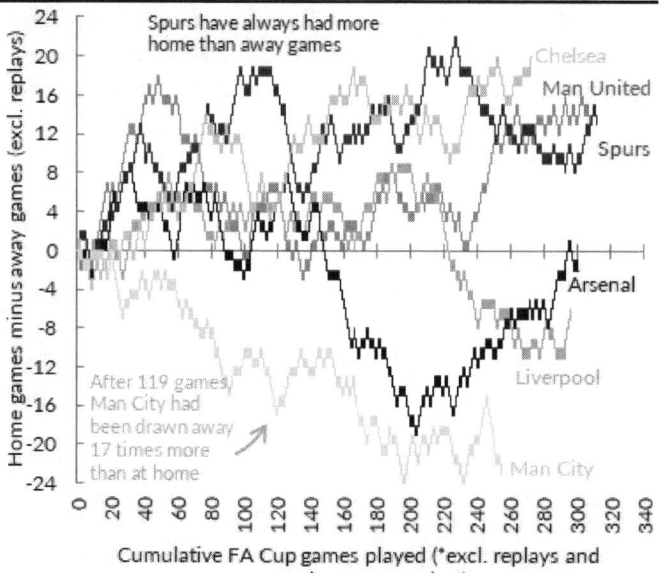

Cumulative FA Cup games played (*excl. replays and neutral-venue matches)

What's also apparent is how streaky good and bad luck can be. As highlighted, Arsenal were once drawn away eight times in a row, 'bettered' only by Spurs' nine times in the 1950s. On the flip side, Manchester United were once drawn at home nine times in a row. When it comes to actual football matches, we refuse to believe we could go half a dozen games in a row where we've been unlucky (or indeed lucky), but that's the true nature of randomness.

The key of course is trying to establish what has been bad (or good) luck and what has been bad (or good) performance. Our Performance League model allows us to do this; it helps cut through the noise and establish whether the current run of results is powered by a random streak of good or bad luck in key incidents, or due to underlying performance.

The league table almost always lies – if luck doesn't even out over 200 matches, it certainly wouldn't over a season.

Attack, Attack, Attack

At half-time during the first leg of their 2017/18 Champions League last 16 tie against Shakhtar Donetsk, Roma led 1-0. Their coach Eusebio di Francesco urged his team to continue attacking; not only had they outshot the Ukranians 9-4, they'd created by far the better chances. Roma had an opportunity to put the tie to bed.

However, within seven second half minutes Shakhtar were level. Roma conceded another with 19 minutes remaining, and could easily have fallen 3-1 behind in injury time. Di Francesco was dismayed. "I told the team to play the second half the way we played the first," he said after the match, "but what I saw on the pitch is that team was happy to defend. We need to work on that."

Roma's players were loss averse; after half time the thought of conceding a goal outbalanced the thought of scoring another. This is our natural instinct, and it's evident across many sports. However, loss aversion often means we don't maximise our chances of winning; in football we find that teams concede at nearly a 20% higher rate when leading by one goal compared to when the scores are level.

Loss aversion means we often undervalue the attacking strategy

Sport	Situation	What we tend to do	What the research suggests leads to more success
Football	Leading by one goal in a tight contest	Sit back and protect our lead	Continue attacking, as teams who do this tend to concede less often
Golf	Putting for birdie	Underhit putts, to avoid having a difficult putt for par	Putt more aggressively; the evidence shows that golfers make more putts this way
American Football	Fourth down	Kick field goals to ensure that points are scored, or punt to keep the opposition close to their own endzone	Going for it, as the benefit and likelihood of achieving a first down outweigh the costs of failing to do so
Twenty20 Cricket	Lost early wickets when batting first	Consolidate and aim to bat the full overs at a lower run rate	Bat aggressively, because there's a big upside to each additional run 'above par'

Quite often the research suggests that we go for what feels to be the 'risky' option. It's true that an adventurous approach can sometimes lead to heavy defeats, but as long as we accept that this is a part of our strategy, and therefore manage the psychological scars that come with it, in the long run we'll actually win more often than under the current status quo.

Roma had to attack in the second leg in order to progress (scraping through with a 1-0 win at home), but their task could have been easier had they been less risk averse in the second half in Kharkiv. Changing human psychology is never the easiest task, but knowing that we aren't alone – and that there is a better way – is a step towards winning more games.

The Perils of Day Trading

Day to day, the market valuation of a stock can fluctuate up and down like a yo-yo. Take Bitcoin right now. Whether the cryptocurrency will be up or down tomorrow is anyone's guess, such is the sentiment volatility towards the relatively new form of exchange.

For traders, it can be addictive. The emotional rollercoaster of something that's unpredictable and easy to measure. While few in football will be trading in the conventional sense, we are day trading in something else: results.

When we win, we think we've cracked it and convince ourselves that it was all within our control. When we lose, it feels like the world is going to implode – we tend to overreact, forgetting that luck often plays a huge role in the outcome of games.

Thankfully we now have objective tools to help us better understand football's short-term 'price movements', but even knowing if the last result was 'fair' will only appease our post-match emotional state. We need a longer-term horizon.

Just as a trader will look for evidence and signals to understand a company's share price (earnings power, net value of their assets, customer satisfaction), similarly a football club must find a mechanism to understand its true underlying long-term performance.

For example, although Bologna lost to SPAL on in Serie A in early March 2018, they would have won the match 47% of the time based on the quality of the performance (SPAL only 18%). Over the past 4 years, Bologna has improved its on-pitch 'share price' by 74 World Super League points, or the equivalent of nearly 12 points over a season.

Bologna's stock has been rising for over three years
World Super League rating, July 2014 to March 2018

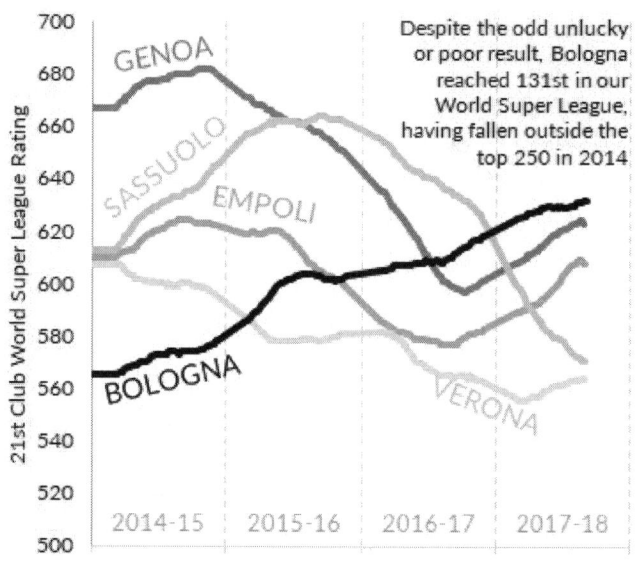

Despite the odd unlucky or poor result, Bologna reached 131st in our World Super League, having fallen outside the top 250 in 2014

In football, results are volatile. They're hard for us to influence and we certainly don't always get what we deserve. It's better, therefore, to focus on how we can positively impact the long-term future of the club and measure that instead.

IV: PLANNING

Confidently Wrong

One of the challenges in prediction (or indeed estimating anything where there are a number of unknowns) is that we all suffer from overconfidence. It's the reason why 93% of drivers think they're better than average, or that project planning often underestimates the real completion time.

Equally, imagine a poll asking the CEOs of a 20-team league what they think their current chances are of relegation and finishing in the top four. The results may look something like this:

Our predictions often overstate our actual chances		
	What do **you** think are **your** chances of...	
Hypothetical respondent	Being relegated?	Finishing in the top four?
Team A	0%	100%
Team B	0%	80%
Team C	0%	80%
Team D	0%	75%
Team E	0%	70%
Team F	0%	55%
Team G	0%	20%
Team H	0%	15%
Team I	5%	5%
Team J	5%	0%
Team K	10%	0%
Team L	15%	0%
Team M	15%	0%
Team N	15%	0%
Team O	20%	0%
Team P	25%	0%
Team Q	25%	0%
Team R	30%	0%
Team S	35%	0%
Team T	50%	0%
Sum Total	250%	500%
Implied Team	2.5 teams	5 teams

Given that the predicted number of relegated teams (2.5) is less than the actual (3), it's clear there's some underestimation going on; either some or all of the teams are overconfident in their ability to stay up. The same applies for finishing in the top four – five teams would not fit into four places.

These small margins may not seem like a big deal, but they can have a significant impact on our plans. Imagine if, by all objective models, Team S's chance of relegation was 50%. Would it be as advisable to be planning a busy January transfer window, when we know the impact of player investment is unpredictable at best? Perhaps, because of misleading results, Team G's 'real' top four chances are closer to 5%, and therefore it may be time to give youth a chance ahead of next season, rather than cling onto a deceptively distant hope.

Prediction isn't easy, but consciously trying to do it better than others will make us better prepared for the future.

How Many Players Do We Need?

Implicit in all decisions around player trading and youth promotion are predictions about the depth of squad needed to compete during the season. Some clubs hope to go deep in all competitions, others are content to prioritise the league.

Given the average footballer's annual pay is a deeply material cost to the club, it makes sense to consult the data to see how many players have been historically needed by club circumstance.

The table below shows the average number of outfield players who played at least 900 minutes – the equivalent of 10 matches – during a season, according to the number of matches that team played in a season.

History shows the depth of squad needed

Average number of players with 900+ minutes in a season
By number of team matches in cup + Europe (Premier League)

		Team playing in Europe?		
		No	Yes	Average*
Team Cup Matches Played	<4	16.8	20.4	17.8
	4 to 5	17.5	19.9	18.0
	6 to 7	17.7	19.4	18.3
	8+	18.5	20.4	19.4
	Average*	17.6	20.0	18.4

*weighted by the number of teams in each bucket

Clubs playing in Europe have typically needed outfield 20 players who can play 900+ minutes; in other words, a high number of players who play a high number of matches. Those not in Europe have needed 2.4 fewer players on average, and even fewer if they have no plans to go far in the cup competitions.

For example, in 2015/16 Leicester City – who played just five cup matches alongside their 38 league games – had just 14 outfield players play 900+ minutes. Meanwhile, Manchester City – who played nine cup matches and reached the Champions League semi-finals – required 21 players to meet this threshold.

Whenever we are planning our team's recruitment, it's worth asking: given our circumstances, how many players do we really need?

A Balancing Act

Squad-building is never a straightforward task; while accounting for size, you also have to consider cost, value and potential future performance.

It's also useful to consider the distribution of performance across the team; how good does our best player have to be relative to our tenth-best player, is there a cost to inequality in talent in the squad, and how does that all relate to our budget?

We can, for example, take a relatively simple metric of goals (below). The top scorer at any given club usually scores about 26% of the team's non-penalty goals, so a Premier League side targeting 7th place – where a team scores just over 50 goals per season – would look for a striker who can deliver about 13 goals per season.

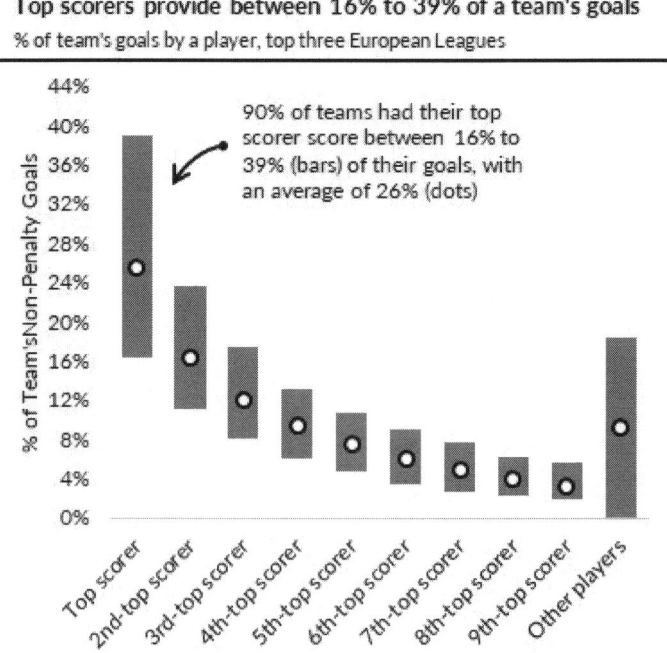

Top scorers provide between 16% to 39% of a team's goals
% of team's goals by a player, top three European Leagues

90% of teams had their top scorer score between 16% to 39% (bars) of their goals, with an average of 26% (dots)

That gives us a starting point for the search process. Would a 13-goal-per-season striker be within budget? What compromise would we have to make elsewhere in the squad if we wanted to reduce our risk in this area?

We have stretched this out further with clubs with whom we work. Our own player contribution metrics provide a perspective on the relative benefit provided by a new player compared to an existing player, and what impact that might have on the club's finances – e.g. player X is worth 2.1 points to us across the season, which should reduce our relegation risk by Y%.

An objective starting point takes us away from generic statements of "player X brings stability to the defence" and "Player Y gives us extra creativity". How much, and can we afford it?

The Leicester City Problem

The sacking of Leicester City manager Claudio Ranieri in February 2017 evoked an understandably fervent response. Many felt that having won the league, the Italian deserved the opportunity to continue his tenure, while others simply felt that in a results business he had failed to assure the club that he was still the right man for the job.

From a boardroom perspective, it's important to properly weigh up the emotional and objective sides of the decision. While acknowledging that a huge amount of thought would have gone into the club's decision, there are a few reflections from Leicester's situation that we can take when making our own major choices:

Consider the long-term impact. Some clubs have actually benefited from a crisis of results, as it allowed them to review the effectiveness of internal processes. Whisper it, but sometimes it may even be better to accept short-term failure for long-term gain.

Treat every decision as a prediction. In making a change, there is an implicit prediction that a new manager would win more points than Ranieri over the final run of games. By writing down exactly how many more we expect, and its projected impact on relegation risk, we can better ground the decision in rationalised subjectivity and be balanced against the enormity of the decision. Better still, find historical benchmarks of similar teams in similar situations to help make the call (though clearly this was a challenge for Leicester).

Understand the reasons for success and failure. Leicester's title run was fuelled in large part by unsustainable factors, including conversion rates at both ends, penalties won, and distribution of goals. Quantifying to what extent these variables were unsustainable, and the expected drop off in 2016/17, would have given a better set of expectations than the one set by the league table.

Rationalise the softer factors, too. In the heat of the season, it's quite easy to get caught up in the mood of events. For example, there was a lot of talk of Ranieri 'losing the dressing room' – but what does that actually mean in terms of relegation chances? Does it affect it by 5%? 20%?

Stay on the lookout. Regardless of how long a manager has been at a club, statistics show that he is on average less than 18 months away from losing his job, so even in the good times there's no reason not to be aware of possible replacements.

The debate over Leicester City's decision shows how, at the time of making a choice, there is often never a right or wrong option. There is, however, a framework for thinking that can reduce the emotion and give us the best chance of being less wrong more of the time.

Taking The Long Road

Being a listed company has many benefits – easy access to capital, for example, and an ability to spread risk among a wider group of investors. But listing can also change a business' priorities as the share price morphs from a useful barometer of market sentiment to a millstone around the neck of CEOs whose performance is judged solely on the whims of that very market.

This encourages short-termism, with measures implemented to satisfy the immediate interests of speculators rather than the long term interests of the company. Of executives surveyed by McKinsey, a whopping 61% said that they would cut discretionary spending in order to avoid missing an earnings target, while 47% would delay starting a new project even if they believed that doing so would reduce long-term value.

The same applies in football where the league table – rather than the share price – is the barometer to which scrutiny is applied. Our position in the table can distract us from investing in initiatives that may deliver indirect long-term value. As such, our focus and budget is disproportionately focused on the players often to the long-term detriment of the club.

For example, these are all things that if invested in now would deliver future benefits to our club:

- Improving our process for allocating scouting resources will deliver sustainable improvements in the quality and value of players that we identify.

- Understanding our financial and performance ROI in player development can help us to get better value from our academy.

- Investing in better ways to remunerate our players and coaching staff may help to improve performance as well as manage financial risk.

- Training our non-playing staff in negotiation may help to get better deals, enabling us to spend our transfer budget more effectively.

Investing in these things may feel peripheral and may not get the juices going, but they will improve the context in which the team operates and have an indirect impact on performance over time.

Returning to the corporate world, McKinsey estimate that firms that were focused on the 'long-term' had revenue and earnings growth rates around 47% and 36% higher respectively than those for whom earnings targets were paramount. Perhaps taking the long road may lead us to a better destination after all.

Breaking The Cycle of Reactivity

Given that the average managerial tenure in the English Football League is just 1.3 years, we should be constantly monitoring the availability and suitability of potential future managers or head coaches.

Even if a club has no immediate intention of changing their manager, coaching turnover is high across football and it pays to be ready for whatever the future may hold. Preparing for all possible scenarios should not be seen as a pessimistic or duplicitous process, but rather an essential element of basic succession planning.

In April 2017 it was announced that Gianfranco Zola had resigned as the manager of Birmingham City. Having slipped from 7th to 20th place under Zola since December 2016, the Italian's departure was not unexpected, but Birmingham appeared to be caught unawares and stranded without a ready replacement. In the rush to appoint a new manager, the Blues turned to Harry Redknapp on a short-term deal for the last three games of the season.

Clearly, with just a handful games remaining, Birmingham didn't have much time to find a replacement for Zola, but there are more proactive steps we can take to avoid being caught out by the departure of a manager.

The implementation of a simple ongoing monitoring process based on defined criteria can help to identify candidates that are suited to our club's playing style and long-term strategy. By meeting criteria that are fully aligned to our wider strategic goals, we can help ensure our decision-making processes are considered, coherent and guided by suitability rather than availability.

Questions we might ask ourselves include:

- Does the candidate play a style of football that suits our club's vision?

- What is the candidate's track record in terms of both results and underlying team performance?

- Does the way the candidate has historically used the transfer market or developed young players align with our strategy?

- How has the candidate performed at previous clubs with similar resource levels?

When we start asking "who's the right fit?" rather than simply "who's available?" we are breaking a cycle of reactivity that has the potential to cause long-term decay. By looking at the bigger picture we free ourselves from the hazards of short-term thinking and establish a platform for sustainable success and the fulfilment of our strategic ambitions.

How to Spend It

When deciding how to improve our squad over the summer, we often have to choose between prioritising defence and attack. In the last four years, clubs have spent just over 75% of transfer fees on midfielders and attackers, which suggests that at the very least clubs are prepared to pay more for attacking talent (perhaps justifiably so, according to our research).

Some clubs spend nine times as much on attacking players
Total transfer fees paid vs % of transfer fees spent on attacking players

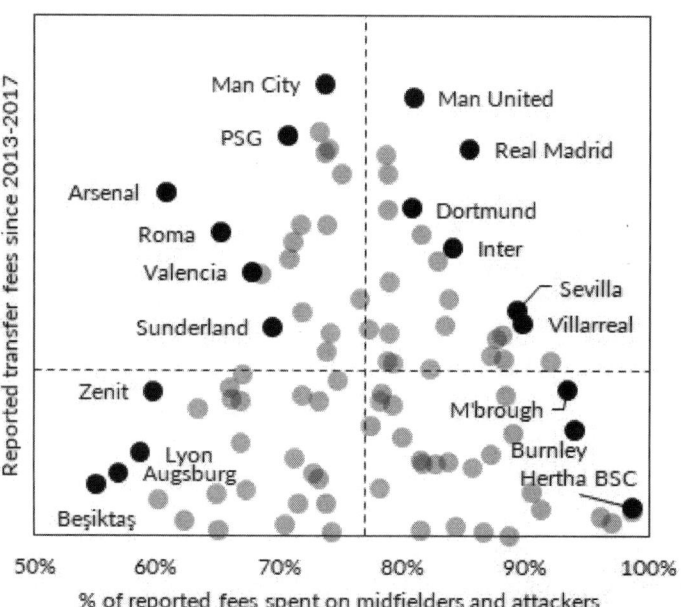

% of reported fees spent on midfielders and attackers

That said, not all teams are close to the average; the chart above allows us to compare the strategies of teams with similar budgets. Manchester United and Real Madrid, for example, have long histories of attacking football, and have focused their attentions on buying players that can uphold these traditions. Meanwhile, nouveau riche clubs Manchester City and PSG have been more inclined to keep funds available for defensive players.

That even the richest clubs don't settle on a common strategy shows the trade-offs and challenges we face. If, for example, the biggest and most obvious improvements are required in defence, then we need to think smartly about spending in attack, and vice versa.

One way clubs can do this is through our new Acquisition module in Evolution, which establishes whether we would be paying above or below the market rate for potential signings. By assigning market values to our transfer targets and identifying undervalued talent, Acquisition mitigates risk and enables us to be more targeted and efficient in terms of the management of our transfer resources.

Each club has its own unique set of circumstances, but having a clear approach to the allocation of our transfer budget – and knowing the expected benefit of each dollar spent – will ensure we maximise our chances of success during the window.

The Rule of Thumb

Following the 2008 financial crash, Bank of England chief economist Andy Haldane looked into what factors caused the crisis. He discovered that breaching the regulations set out in Basel II – a complex 347-page document that attempted to ensure banks remained safe – proved a less effective predictor of failure than a crude rule of thumb: highly leveraged firms were more likely to fail.

In other words, Haldane concluded, "less is more".

We could learn from this approach in football. Like Haldane, we have a few rules of thumb we use with boardrooms:

- A league table ranked by goal difference is a better indicator of quality than one ranked by points.

- A good manager can improve your team by about five points per season over an average manager.

- If you're a relegation candidate, a defensive setup gives you a better chance of survival.

- Late-season senior debuts often reflect poorer planning, and lead to fewer future opportunities for the player.

- Players bought from stronger teams (according to our World Super League model) are more successful.

These rules of thumb create a starting point for decisions that require us to compute a lot of information. Decisions like: should we change our manager? Or: where should we prioritise our squad expenditure?

While recognising that smart clubs have reliable and often complex processes that enable better decision-making, sometimes a simple rule of thumb can set us off on the right path.

The Sport We Think We Know

We recently put the following questions to our team at 21st Club:

> 1. What % of the time does a player who has scored one goal go on to score two or more in a game?

> 2. What % of red cards are the result of two yellow cards?

> 3. What % of throw-ins are taken in the attacking half of the field?

> 4. What % of all incoming loan deals are defenders and goalkeepers?

Though the questions are incredibly simple – and about a sport we've each followed religiously for decades – no one got all the questions right to within the margin of error.

This exercise in itself is a little trivial, but it does show that we don't always have the best intuitive grasp of this sport that we all know and love.

And because of that, we might not have the best intuitive grasp of more important questions, like:

- What are the chances our record signing plays over 50% of minutes?

- What % of teams in our position avoid relegation?

- What is the typical maximum improvement in points per game for clubs that change their manager mid-season?

- What is the probability one of our under-18s provides a financial return on investment?

The answers to these questions can influence multi-million dollar decisions, and yet we often rely on our intuition to guide us – the same intuition that isn't quite certain about the pattern of throw ins even though we've watched tens of thousands in our lifetime.

Objective information can point us in the right direction and ensure that we're that little bit smarter about the sport we think we know.

1: 12% (7%, 17%); 2. 54% (49%, 59%); 3. 57% (52%, 62%); 4. 33% (28%, 38%)

The Right Head Coach

Barely two months into the 2017/18 season, ten men had already lost their jobs as head coach or manager of clubs in England, Spain, Germany and Italy's top divisions. This level of turnover is now an accepted part of the game, despite it being a clear inefficiency.

Recruiting a head coach is a tougher task than recruiting a player, because a coach's skills are less explicit and measurable. However, when we work with clubs we try to mitigate risk by first finding managers in our database who have a track record in improving the teams they have led. This is looking beyond win percentage and results and understanding the impact they had on underlying performance. Then, we can try and understand if their historical playing style suits the profile of the players in our squad. Ideally, we can find managers who fulfil both criteria – as Ralph Hasenhüttl clearly did for RB Leipzig, below.

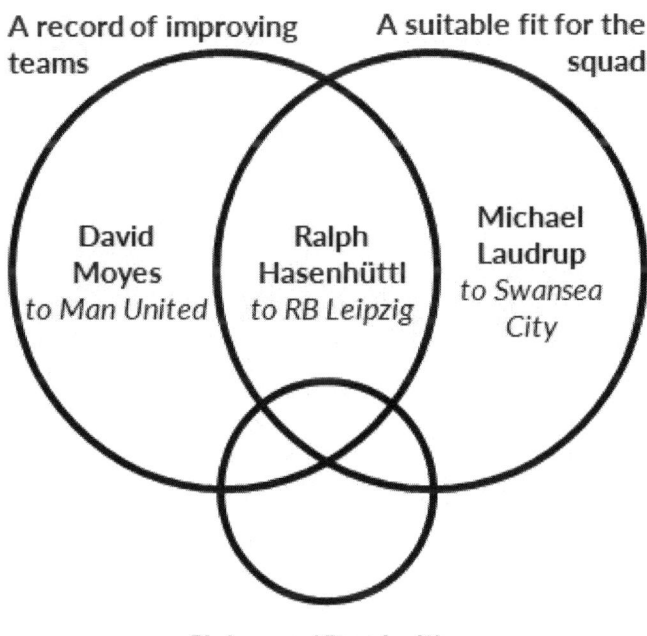

Finally, smart clubs will do their due diligence on other factors they feel are important too; perhaps they want a manager who is used to managing international dressing rooms, or a coach who has maximised playing time of his new (and often costly) recruits. Better still, they will try and understand what factors really matter for success.

This process is merely the starting point before softer considerations come into play, but at the very least it will produce a list of people that are more likely to replicate the success they had at previous clubs. We know the best managers can be worth 10 points per season; it's time we implement the processes to reflect this.

The Rise and Fall of Chile

Between 2013 and 2016, Chile were one of the most watchable and successful teams in world football. From qualifying for the 2014 World Cup with five wins in their last six matches, to being the width of the crossbar away from knocking out Brazil in the tournament proper, to consecutive Copa América triumphs, Chile were a relative underdog that became a global force.

2017 was far less successful for *La Roja*. A meek showing at the Confederations Cup was followed by a collapse in form that saw them miss out on the 2018 World Cup.

Chile's biggest problem was that they were unable to refresh their squad; seven of their core players at the 2010 World Cup were still core players at the 2017 Confederations Cup, ageing to an average of 30 years and 7 months in the process.

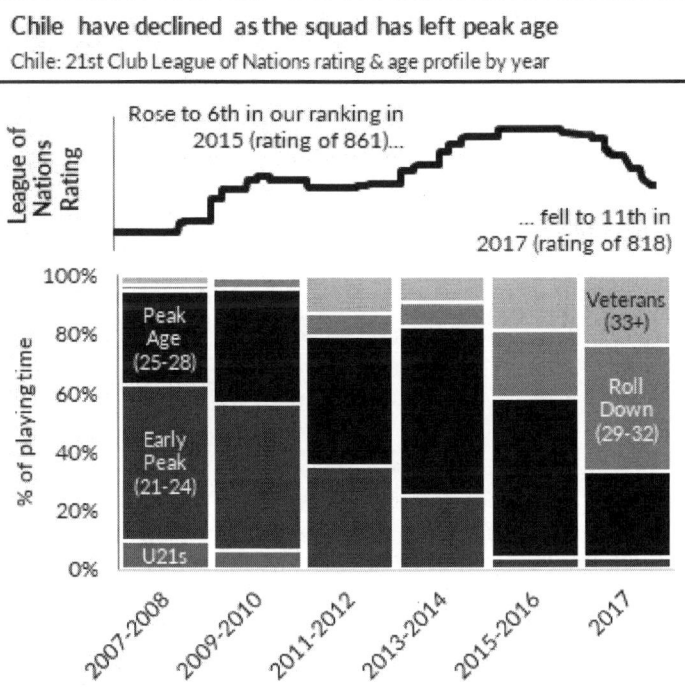

Chile have declined as the squad has left peak age

Chile: 21st Club League of Nations rating & age profile by year

Chile's evolution from young and dynamic to ageing and slow is a useful reminder of how having a squad that is mainly peak age is a key factor for success. We often overvalue historic performances of successful players when trying to predict their future output, failing to appreciate that time marches on until after the event.

For many clubs their position in football's 'food chain' means creating peak-age squads is easier said than done. However, being on top of squad planning and ensuring you have the profile you need for success is an underrated and achievable source of competitive edge.

As for Chile, after all of their success, a poor squad profile means it is now a long road back to the top.

Finding Marco

We are beginning to appreciate the substantial impact that a good manager or head coach may have on our prospects over a season, and those that have had high-profile success are becoming increasingly desirable. Take Marco Silva for example, who was subject to a £10m offer to buy him out during his time at Watford. His popularity is understandable in light of the impact that he has had on both of the teams that he has managed in the Premier League.

Silva's performance, like Mauricio Pochettino's before him, is well known, but the exciting thing is that there are many other managers who have had a similar or even bigger impact on their teams who are rarely, if ever, talked about. The main difference is that they have done this outside of the division that the boardrooms know best.

There are metrics that help identify other Marco Silvas
Head coach performance vs resources and predecessor, 400 tenures, 2013-

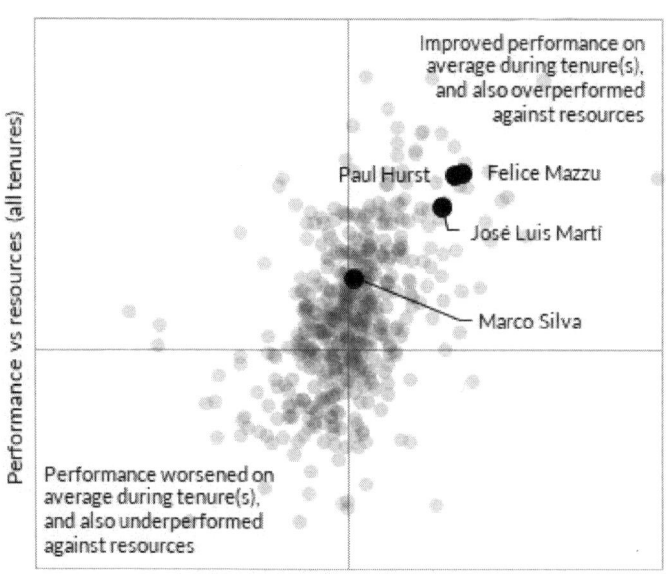

That these managers are rarely talked about is due, in part, to the value placed on having managed in our league. Our own research at 21st Club suggests that league-specific experience is overrated and that in reality there is no correlation, for example, between experience in the Premier League and success. Sir Alex Ferguson, Arsène Wenger, Jürgen Klopp, Pep Guardiola, José Mourinho, Mauricio Pochettino and Marco Silva had all, at some stage, never managed in the Premier League. As Captain Chesley "Sully" Sullenberger said sometime following the emergency landing of US Airways Flight 1549 on the Hudson River, "Everything is unprecedented until it happens for the first time".

The other reason that we don't notice strong managerial performance outside of our own league is that we simply don't look. The sheer number of potential candidates makes monitoring their performance a daunting task. Yet we are increasingly working with forward-thinking clubs across Europe who are keen to explore what the wider market has to offer. Discussions around the club's aspirations, requirements and playing philosophy enable us to narrow the field through creating managerial performance indices which rule out candidates who are either a poor fit, or are not performing effectively relative to the resources at their disposal.

Ultimately, identifying high-performing candidates from across the continent where there is less competition for their signature helps us to acquire affordable talent so that if Marco isn't an option, at least we can find others like him.

The Cost of January

The January transfer window is well-known to be a chaotic period, with circumstance rather than planning being a key driver of activity.

The general perception is that a good window can turn performance around; we can all think of examples of teams that spent significantly on new players and saw an improvement in results. The bigger picture, however, shows that the relationship between spending and success is weak at best. There are plenty of teams who ostensibly strengthened their squad, but ended up doing worse after January – and vice versa.

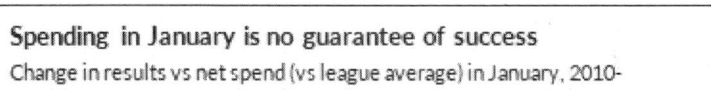

Spending in January is no guarantee of success
Change in results vs net spend (vs league average) in January, 2010-

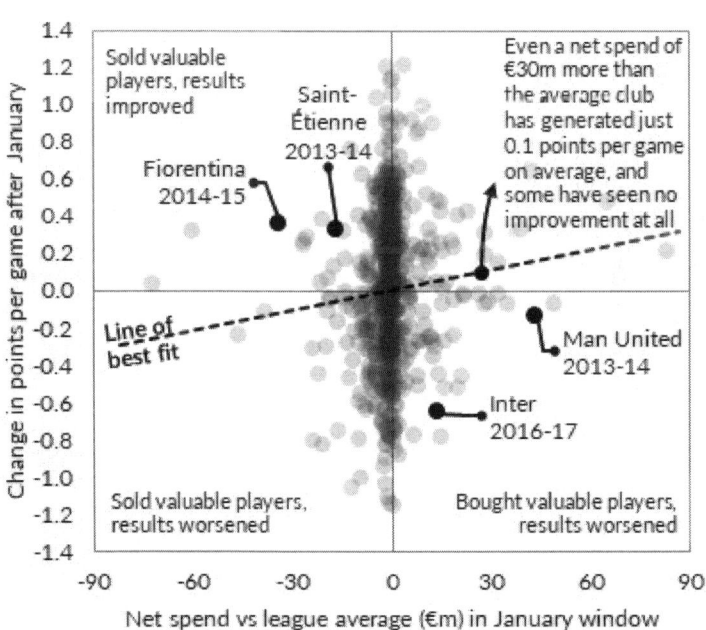

Net spend vs league average (€m) in January window

If our club does need a boost in January, it is useful to know that brute force spending alone is unlikely to work, given it might only be worth one or two extra points if we follow historical trends. In order to outperform history, we have to think differently to the clubs that created it.

This can be hard given the need to execute quickly. However, tools like Acquisition enable immediate access to the most important information. Processes that are evidence-based and everyone has bought into can only help, too. History suggests there is little value for money in January – but maybe it's because we haven't got it quite right yet.

Opportunity Knocks

It seems hard to believe that only a few months ago, Nick Foles was just another forgotten NFL quarterback mooching around on the sidelines waiting for his chance. In February 2018, the newly-crowned Super Bowl MVP spearheaded the Philadelphia Eagles to victory against the much-fancied New England Patriots, having grasped the opportunity only when the team's supposedly superior starter got sidelined through injury.

On the same weekend, across the pond in Cardiff, a Welsh rugby team decimated by injuries comfortably overcame Scotland with a crop of players who would otherwise likely have been ignored. Suddenly these relatively unknown players have become first choice, deservedly retaining their starting places for the next match against England despite the return of more established internationals.

While such stories seem romantic and unlikely, we actually don't need to look too hard in any sport to find a Nick Foles fairytale – a player who came to prominence only because of an unexpected opportunity. Marcus Rashford is one of football's Foles' of course, having established himself at Manchester United and England on the back on an injury crisis at his club.

The truth is that in most sports opportunity is often the result of necessity rather than strategy. And understandably so. Just like the NFL is reluctant to give its next generation of players a chance when there are so few matches in the season, football's head coaches can also be forgiven for not risking the younger fringe players – it's their reputation and job on the line, after all. Inevitably we're told that "they're not ready" or "not good enough" to step up.

Herein lies one of football's biggest dilemmas: balancing the long-term need to increase the asset value in the squad portfolio by affording more minutes to fringe players, with the short-term need to secure results. It is not an easy paradox to reconcile, but there is hope.

We can learn from the past to inform the future by taking inspiration from the likes of Foles and Rashford. Those anecdotes should encourage us to think differently about opportunity and succession planning, while data can also reveal misconceptions about the perceived risk of giving peripheral players a chance.

Sometimes "not good enough" really means "not prepared to risk it". Yet these real stories and data suggest that perhaps we should be more willing. Often we have more strength in depth than our head coaches or indeed our own fears would have us believe. Or, as Foles himself put it after winning the Super Bowl: "I think the big thing is don't be afraid to fail".

When He Leaves the Building

One of the things that makes sport different to other industries is a sporting organisation's dependency on a relatively small number of individuals. In the UK for example, a large 'normal' business generating £200m+ in turnover will employ over 1,500 people on average. A Premier League club with the same income might have a workforce that is one-fifth the size of this.

In most cases, the importance of a star footballer to a club outweighs even the most celebrated CEOs in a 'normal' business. A top player might be worth 5 points – and therefore impact expected revenues by over 5% – per season to a club, whereas Apple's share price fell just 0.7% in the day after Steve Jobs' resignation in 2011.

The head coach is another key part of the business, especially if they've been at the club a while. During this time, he (and it almost always is a 'he') develops a number of processes – from training sessions, to player development, to cultural management – that are in danger of leaving the building when the time comes for him to depart. The need to mitigate key person risk is less significant in other industries outside of football, because there are a greater number of employees involved in building and running operational processes.

The data suggests that this departure of knowledge from football clubs does happen from time to time; the chart below plots clubs who in the last few years lost a head coach who had been at the club for over eight years. While some clubs (e.g. Leioa, New England) kicked on from the foundations laid by their long-term head coach, many others have seen performance deteriorate over the years (e.g. Rubin Kazan), or taken longer to reach that level again (e.g. Manchester United).

Clubs don't always kick on when a long-time coach leaves

Change in performance after a coach with an 8+ year tenure leaves

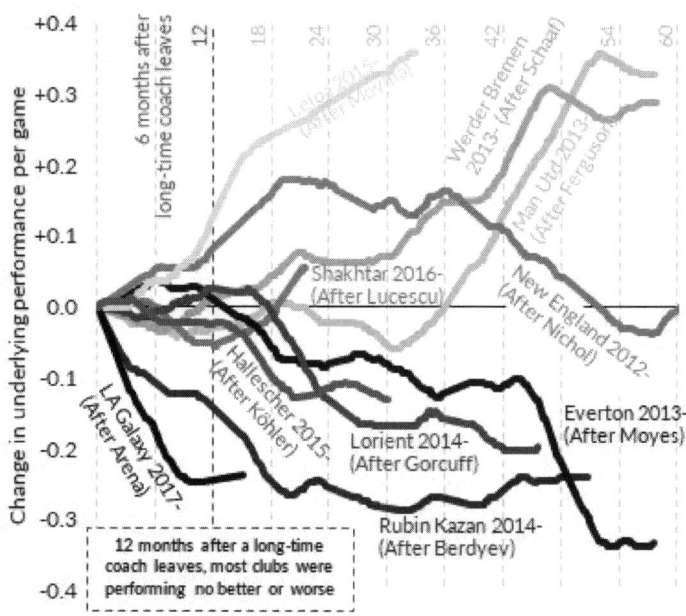

While it's perhaps unreasonable to expect successors to exceed the performance levels set by someone who has become a club legend, we can always be better at making sure the previous coach's ideas and processes are retained as the club's own intellectual property.

Indeed, this applies to any aspect in the running of our club. Is our Head of Academy's process for tracking the development of our young players just in his head and laptop, or is it a physical part of the club? Can we maintain our record in recruiting undervalued talent when our sporting director leaves the club?

Sustainable success is hard to build in a unique industry, but that's no reason to let knowledge leave the building without first making it a part of our club's fabric.

Bibliography

Books

21st Club, *Changing the Conversation: 21st Club Presents a Collection of Insights for Football Club Boardrooms* (CreateSpace, 2016)

Kahneman, Daniel, *Thinking, Fast and Slow* (Penguin, 2012)

Tetlock, Philip and Gardner, Dan, *Superforecasters: The Art and Science and Prediction* (Random House, 2016)

Newspapers

The Guardian

The Sunday Times

Websites

https://www2.deloitte.com/uk/en/pages/sports-business-group/articles/deloitte-football-money-league.html

https://www.mckinsey.com

https://medium.com/@buster

https://www.reddit.com/user/zonination

Films

Jerry Maguire (TriStar Pictures, 1996)

Other

The Bill Simmons Podcast

EVOLUTION

The smart way to plan for the future

Software for football club boardrooms

26357712R00088

Printed in Great Britain
by Amazon